PREACHING THE PARABLES

Series II, Cycle B

WILLIAM E. KEENEY

CSS Publishing Co., Inc.
Lima, Ohio

Copyright © 1996 by
CSS Publishing Company, Inc.
Lima, Ohio

Scripture quotations are from the *New Revised Standard Version of the Bible*, copyright 1989, by the Division of Christian Education of the National Council of the Churches of Christ in the USA. Used by permission.

Library of Congress Cataloging-in-Publication Data

Keeney, William E. (William Echard), 1922-
    Preaching the parables. Cycle B / William E. Keeney.
       p.   cm.
    ISBN 0-7880-0825-0 (pbk.)
    1. Jesus Christ—Parables. 2. Bible. N. T. Gospels—Homiletical use. 3. Preaching.
I. Title.
BT375.2.K3863   1996
251—dc20

                 96-5305
                 CIP

This book is available in the following formats, listed by ISBN:
0-7880-0825-0 Book
0-7880-0826-9 IBM 3 1/2 computer disk
0-7880-0827-7 Macintosh computer disk
0-7880-0828-5 Sermon Prep

PRINTED IN U.S.A.

Dedication

To preachers who had special influence on my path to ministry:

Dwight L. Stevenson, the first preacher I remember
Thomas Pletcher, the first to suggest I go into the ministry
Artemus Porter Goodwin, a Baptist who showed friendship in WW II
Jesse N. Smucker, a Mennonite who attracted me to Mennonites
William Beahm, Church of the Brethren, an inspiring teacher

Editor's Note Regarding The Lectionary

During the past two decades there has been an attempt to move in the direction of a uniform lectionary among various Protestant denominations.

•Lectionary Uniformity

Preaching on the same scripture lessons every Sunday is a step in the right direction of uniting Christians of many faiths. If we are reading the same scriptures together we may also begin to accomplish other achievements. Our efforts will be strengthened through our unity.

•Christian Unity

Beginning with Advent 1995 The Evangelical Lutheran Church in America dropped its own lectionary schedule and adopted the Revised Common Lectionary.

•ELCA Adopts Revised Common Lectionary

Reflecting this change, resources published by CSS Publishing Company put their major emphasis on the Revised Common Lectionary texts.

Table Of Contents

Introduction

Storytelling is popular for all ages and in various cultures. Children love stories. They will ask that the same stories be read or told over and over again. Even though they cannot read, they often will correct the reader if one little detail is left out or changed. Years later they will remember the stories and may be able to repeat them almost verbatim. Groups of adults organize to tell stories and put on programs to share them with others. Some people repeat favorite stories over and over again.

The popularity of the long-running radio program "A Prairie Home Companion" is in large part due to the stories Garrison Keillor spins in the monologue. The fact that it is radio and not television may at first seem strange. It is probably the very fact that the listeners must visualize the story in their own heads that is part of the attraction.

Stories are popular because they mirror life in a memorable form. They present in specific experiences universal realities about human nature and the world. They tickle the imagination and arouse creativity in people. They often provide morals which are easily remembered and applied later in life.

Parables are stories which present some aspect of the good news of God's kingdom. They usually are brief and intended to make a single point. Sometimes they are not much more than an extended metaphor. They may at times be longer, more complex and become allegories. The parables are reflections of the culture at the time when they were told. They use familiar events for those people. They may need explanation or some translation to make first century culture meaningful to twentieth century culture.

To use the parables a sermon should transport the hearers into the mind and spirit of Christ. Then they may become vehicles to carry the gospel message to the people. Such sermons can be helpful by instilling in the minds of the people a universal truth in a story that is easy to remember and apply when the situation is relevant to the parable.

To be effective in preaching from the parables, a person has to engage in disciplined study. The first step is to read the scripture passage in its fuller context and to understand the single point or the more complex message intended by the parable. The literary study of the parable needs to be considered. Often it is more like reading poetry than straight history or other discursive writing. One should not be intimidated by allegory because of the abuses of the form sometimes in the past. Usually when allegory is used the explanations accompanying it provide safeguards against fancy flights of the imagination which lead one astray from the real message. One needs to experience the spiritual reality and communicate it with integrity to its original intent and purpose.

Then one ought to meditate on the meaning and let the Spirit open its truth for the needs of today. The situation of the members of the congregation should be brought to mind. They are struggling with troubles and difficulties. They may need support and encouragement. The parables can be used to help illuminate, inspire and edify the congregation if they speak to the condition in which the listeners find themselves. Be confident that if you search diligently, seek guidance, and wait patiently for the Spirit to speak, you will find your way directed.

The material provided in this book is not intended to give you complete sermons or a finished product. Rather the suggestions are intended to "prime the pump," that is, to start your own imagination and help you understand the parables more fully. Possible directions to go in the use of the parables are also offered but need to be tested to relate to the particular place where you and your congregation are found.

Cycle B has seven parables. Three are from the Gospel according to Mark. Mark does not include extensive sections on the teachings of Jesus. He reports actions in a chronological fashion to give you the account of what Jesus did. Even the parables which have parallels in Matthew and Luke tend to be shorter than those versions. Matthew and Luke elaborate and include additional details.

Because Mark has so few parables and only a couple that are peculiar to Mark, the Lectionary includes materials from the Gospel according to John. Four of the selections for this cycle are from John. They often are more of the nature of extended metaphors (I am the Good Shepherd) or of allegories than the form of the parables found in the synoptic gospels. John has certain themes that are introduced in the first chapter. They are then repeated, expanded and demonstrated whether by action of Jesus or his lengthy discourses.

A good exercise to seek to enter into the figures used by Mark or John would be to try to find some common everyday images from twentieth century culture that would communicate the same message but be more part of the experience of modern Christians.

May you receive the blessing of the Spirit as you experience the message of the parables and as you mediate the mind and presence of Christ to others in your preaching.

1. The Fig Tree Lesson

Mark 13:24-37

24"But in those days, after that suffering,
the sun will be darkened,
and the moon will not give its light,
25and the stars will be falling from heaven,
and the powers in the heavens will be shaken.
26Then they will see 'the Son of Man coming in clouds'
with great power and glory. 27Then he will send out the
angels, and gather his elect from the four winds, from the
ends of the earth to the ends of heaven.

28"From the fig tree learn its lesson: as soon as its
branch becomes tender and puts forth its leaves, you know
that summer is near. 29So also, when you see these things
taking place, you know that he is near, at the very gates.
30Truly I tell you, this generation will not pass away until
all these things have taken place. 31Heaven and earth
will pass away, but my words will not pass away.

32"But about that day or hour no one knows, neither
the angels in heaven, nor the Son, but only the Father.
33Beware, keep alert; for you do not know when the time
will come. 34It is like a man going on a journey, when he
leaves home and puts his slaves in charge, each with his
work, and commands the doorkeeper to be on the watch.
35Therefore, keep awake — for you do not know when the
master of the house will come, in the evening, or at
midnight, or at cockcrow, or at dawn, 36or else he may
find you asleep when he comes suddenly. 37And what I
say to you I say to all: Keep awake."

We were traveling in the dark. The route number told us to
make a turn north as we merged with another major highway. Then

we relaxed and in a very short time missed the sign that told us to turn east again. In the dark and not watching carefully on an unfamiliar road, we missed the sign. Sometime later we realized that we were not seeing signs for our route and the exit signs pointed toward unfamiliar towns. We realized that we had not read the signs carefully enough. It cost us an hour of travel and added about fifty miles to our trip. Fortunately, missing the signs was only inconvenient and added cost. It was not disastrous.

People are advised to look for signs of cancer. A lump, if detected early, may be removed and the survival rate is increasingly better. If we miss the signs or ignore them, however, it can be tragic.

In the late twenties and thirties the international community did not read the signs of what was happening in Germany and Japan. The consequences were World War II and the concentration camps with millions of deaths and untold suffering and destruction. Reading the signs properly and early may have forestalled the war and saved many lives.

The parable of the budding fig tree is Jesus' response to a question about signs. Jesus warns people about the dire consequences if they do not read the signs and respond in time to be prepared to avoid catastrophe.

Context

Context of the Day

The day is the first Sunday of Advent. It begins a new church year. The day begins the period of preparation for the birth of Jesus. By using the parable for the first Sunday of Advent, people can be alerted to know the signs of the coming birth of Jesus as they were given to people at the time. Some used them for rejoicing and fulfillment of their longings; Herod saw the signs as occasion for threat and fear.

The use of the parable can point beyond the birth to the end of Jesus' life and on to the hope and longing for the fulfillment of history and the kingdom of God. Each of us is given signs in our

14

life of the need to respond to Christ's call so that our life does not end in disaster. We can also read the signs where we are called to work in history to accomplish God's purposes more fully.

Some may need to note that in the revision of the Lectionary, this parable has been moved from Proper 28 to Advent 1. If you are still following the earlier lectionary order you may want to postpone the use of it until that Sunday in the calendar year for Cycle B.

Context in Mark

Chapter 13 of Mark is frequently referred to as the Little Apocalypse. It contains the vivid imagery and picturesque language of other apocalyptic writings, such as is found in Isaiah, Daniel, Matthew 13, Revelation, and some of the noncanonical books.

Apocalyptic writings look forward to the final events of history. They look behind the events of history and also look beyond them. They often use poetic language as they seek to express certainties and hopes that are beyond the normal human experience.

The particular setting for the parable in Mark is when Jesus was sitting on the Mount of Olives (Mark 13:3). Jesus was looking across the valley to the temple area. He could be aware of two events in the future. It was commonly believed that God would judge the nations at the foot of the Mount of Olives. He also anticipated his death in Jerusalem. The disciples were still refusing to read the signs of the growing opposition that would lead to Jesus' crucifixion.

Context of the Lectionary

The First Lesson. (Isaiah 64:1-9) The section begins with a plea for God to come down and disclose the power that shows the character of the true God. It ends with a plea for understanding and that God will not be exceedingly angry with the people.

The Second Lesson. (1 Corinthians 1:3-9) Paul gives thanks that the grace of God given in Jesus Christ has enriched the

Corinthians. They still look forward to the revealing of the Lord Jesus Christ. He calls them to be strengthened so that they will be blameless on that day.

Gospel. (Mark 13:24-37) The passage closes with an admonition to be awake and watchful so that those who read the signs are prepared for the coming event that may be imminent. The exact time when it will occur is uncertain.

Psalm. (Psalm 80:1-7, 17-19) As in the first lesson for the day, the psalmist calls for the intervention of the Shepherd of Israel to stir himself and restore them. It is followed by a plea that God not be angry with the people as is evident from the way the people's enemies scorn and laugh at them. The final verses look for an agent of God who will bring them back to obedience to God and save them.

Context of Related Scriptures

Parallel accounts of Mark 13:24-37 are found in Matthew 24:29-44 and Luke 21:25-31.

> Isaiah 13:10 — A somewhat different version of Mark 13:24-25.
> Isaiah 34:4-5 — Another description of cosmic disorders followed by judgment.
> Daniel 7 — A chapter filled with apocalyptic imagery.
> Daniel 7:13 — A reference to the Son of Man (like a human being) coming with the clouds of heaven.
> Joel 2:30—3:3 — Portents from heaven leading to judgment but also the salvation of Jerusalem and the gathering of the nations.
> Zechariah 2:6-13 — A warning to flee the land followed by the direct intervention of the Lord against the enemies.
> Matthew 12:38-42 — The only sign given to the scribes and Pharisees who asked for one is the sign of Jonah.
> Matthew 13:41 — The people of Nineveh rising up at the judgment.

Matthew 25:13 — Jesus admonishes the disciples to keep awake, for the day and hour is uncertain.

2 Thessalonians 1:7-10 — The Lord Jesus is revealed from heaven in judgment.

Revelation 19-20 — Apocalyptic imagery of the final judgment.

Content

Precis (Mark 13:24-37)

The passage opens with a free quotation by Jesus of Old Testament images of cosmic events leading to the coming of the Son of Man. Jesus then tells the lesson of the fig tree that gives a sign that summer is coming when it puts forth its leaves. The disciples are admonished to heed the signs of God's judgment. Given the uncertainty of the time of the cataclysmic events leading to the judgment, the disciples are urged to be awake and alert constantly.

Thesis: Be awake and alert for the signs of God's activity that leads to judgment.

Theme: Read the signs of God's coming in power.

Key Words in the Parable

1. "The Son of Man." (v. 26) The divine agent who comes from God to exercise judgment between the good and evil.

2. "Coming in the Clouds." (v. 26) Indications that the Son of Man is more than a human being. He is endowed with the full glory and power of God to carry out judgment.

3. "Gather His Elect." (v. 27) The prevailing view in Judaism was that all the Jews, the chosen people, would be gathered in Jerusalem at the final judgment. This reference does not restrict the chosen people to the Jews but includes the universally scattered elect of God.

4. "Summer is Near." (v. 28) The fig tree sends out new leaves at the approach of summer. You don't need a calendar to tell you when summer is coming. Nature sends its own signals.

5. "Summer ... Gates." (vv. 28, 29) Here is a play on words. Summer in Greek is *theros*; gate in Greek is *thuros*.

6. "Near, at the Very Gates." (v. 29) Just as you know that summer is at the gate of the orchard when the fig tree sends out shoots, so you know God's judgment is near when cosmic events occur.

7. "My Words Will not Pass Away." (v. 31) In the midst of the uncertainty of history, the teachings of Jesus remain certain.

8. "That Day or Hour No One Knows." (v. 32) If even the angels and Jesus do not know the time of the Parousia, how much more should we not engage in idle speculation about it.

9. "Evening ... Midnight ... Cockcrow ... Dawn." (v. 35) The use of the divisions of time is according to Roman customs, also known to the Greeks. The night was divided into four parts by them as opposed to the Hebrew division into three parts.

10. "Find you Asleep." (v. 36) Since this occurred on the Mount of Olives prior to the Passover week, this probably has echoes of the memory that the disciples were asleep when Jesus was praying in Gethsemane. They were unprepared when the arrest came.

Contemplation

Issues and Insights

1. What Power? We speak of many kinds of power. Military power, political power, water power, electrical power, mechanical power and the power of the sword. In the face of these kinds of power Jesus seemed to represent powerlessness. He consorted with those whom most people would consider to be outside of power. His opponents represented the ruling leaders of his time, both religiously and politically. They were the so-called "power elite."

Yet the scriptures talk about the power of God. Jesus speaks of the Son of Man coming in glory and power. What kind of power does God exercise or represent in the world? What kind of power did Jesus exercise when he was not part of either the religious or the political governing forces of his day? Is power found in righteousness and justice? Does power reside in moral force? Is the word more powerful than the sword?

Does God's power work mighty deeds because people have an innate sense of what is true, right and fair? If enough people recognize that God's way of love as incarnated in Jesus of Nazareth is the true meaning of human life, will that grow into a power that will overcome the power of evil in human society?

Do we believe that God is active both in history and in nature? We have a difficult time in our scientific culture believing that the power of nature has any purposefulness to it. It seems to operate without regard to any qualities such as right or wrong, justice or injustice, evil or good. Yet nature does seem on balance to support life and goodness rather than death and destruction.

How do we read the signs of power and embrace the way of Christ in love, reconciliation and redemption? Do we act as though these are the real sources of power while appearing to the world to be irrelevant and powerless?

2. Expecting the Parousia. The timing and nature of the Parousia is an issue that already caused concern in the New Testament church and raises questions among commentators yet today. The passage for today seems to suggest that Jesus expected his return as the glorified Son of Man within the generation then living. (See Mark 13:28-30.) If that is so, then two explanations of what that meant are offered.

The first explanation is that Jesus was mistaken about his anticipation of the immediate future. That view would say that his mistaken expectation demonstrates his true humanity. He did affirm that the timing of such future events was unknown to him or to any other agency of God. The events are to occur but they are yet to come. We live in anticipation but with uncertainty as to when it will occur. Our life should be lived in such a manner that we are prepared for the Parousia whenever and however it may happen.

A second explanation would be that Jesus was referring to the presence of Christ in a personal form after his crucifixion. The cosmic events occurred when the sky was darkened and the curtain of the temple was rent in two at his death. Jesus came in a personal way after his death, first to the disciples in his post-resurrection appearances. He came also to Paul on the Damascus road. He appears to other believers when they sense and respond to his presence in their life.

As to the future end of history, we live in trust that God's wisdom will provide for any eventual outcome. We live in such a way as to rely on God's grace and mercy. If the judgment comes with the end of our life on earth or in some cataclysmic final event, we face such outcomes in confidence and hope.

3. Active Waiting. Jesus never expected that his followers would simply engage in passive waiting for some divine intervention into human affairs. In the presence of human need he admonished his followers to be active in preaching the gospel, teaching people all the things he had commanded, and healing those who were hurting.

Jesus taught that a cup of cold water given in his name, feeding the hungry, clothing the naked, and ministering to the sick, the prisoner, the widow and orphan in their distress were activities which would show the presence of God's kingdom. He expected that his disciples would be awake and watching constantly by carrying out the mission that he himself had fulfilled in the days of his flesh.

Homily Hints

1. Triumph Beyond Tragedy. (vv. 24-27) In the midst of the world's tragedies Jesus expected his followers to be meeting the needs of people, bringing God's triumph out of human and natural tragedies.

    A. The Tragedy of Natural Events. When nature goes on a rampage in floods, earthquakes, hurricanes, tornadoes and volcanic eruptions people suffer. Christians then have a responsibility and opportunity to show God's mercies by meeting the human need consequent to such disasters.

    B. Problems and Challenges. When Jesus met people in need, such as the woman at the well in John 4, the man born blind in John 9, or the epileptic boy in Mark 9, Matthew 17 and Luke 9, he did not look upon them as problem people. He saw them as opportunities to witness to God's power and grace.

    C. The Expectation of the Kingdom. Cosmic disorders which may have tragic consequences are opportunities to show the mercy and grace of God and to move beyond tragedy to triumph.

2. Great Power and Glory. (v. 26) God uses the disorders to shake up people and show his power and glory.

    A. Nature Shakes. They give evidence of the power God has invested in creation.

    B. Worldly Power Shaken. God moves in history to accomplish his purposes. Evil rulers exercise punishment but are also in turn afflicted with the rod of iron in judgment.

    C. Personal Power Shaken. God uses the disturbances in people's lives to awaken them to the need for repentance and salvation.

3. Reading the Signs. (vv. 28-29) We learn to read signs from various sources and can anticipate what is coming because of them. Can we also read the signs of the Spirit?

    A. The Signs of Nature. We read the signs for life and growth, but also of death.

    B. The Signs of Society. We read the signs of health and progress, but also of decay and decline.

C. The Signs of the Spirit. Some signs point to hope and glory while others are signs of warning. Which will we heed?

4. The Power of Endurance. (v. 31)

A. The Enduring Word. Biblical wisdom has withstood the test of time. It has awakened persons in many cultures and endured through centuries despite all the forces arrayed against it.

B. The Enduring Christian. Despite various attempts to suppress Christianity by the Romans, the Soviet Union, the Chinese Communists and others, Christianity has persisted through Christians who have endured faithfully in spite of persecution and suffering.

C. The Enduring God. The God of Abraham, Isaac and Jacob has become the God and Father of Jesus Christ. He can now become my God as well.

5. What Are You Waiting For? (vv. 32-37)

A. Waiting for Yourself. Awake to opportunities for fulfillment in the image of God.

B. Waiting for History. Watch for the propitious moments in history and then act to make a difference for the kingdom of God.

C. Waiting for the Church. Observe how the church can more faithfully witness to the kingdom of God and support those possibilities.

D. Waiting for God. At times we simply have to wait and let God act, in confidence and hope that God will do so.

Contact

Points of Contact

1. Christians Recognize the Signs. Christians read various signs of God's Spirit at work in the world. A first type of sign is in their own lives. Awareness of sin and failure in our own lives brings us to an understanding of the need for a power outside ourselves.

We realize that in our own strength we are insufficient. We are alienated from God and that leads to alienation from others around us. Ultimately we recognize that we are even alienated from our true selves. We yield ourselves to the power of Christ's spirit to redeem us and enable us to come to our real self in him.

The second type of sign is in the society of which we are a part. Having the model of the kingdom of heaven as a realm of mercy, grace and righteousness, we see where society is in need of redemption. Empowered by God we are called to witness to the society by working to change that which is contrary to God's intention for people living together. We do it both by the word of warning and also by the deeds of mercy and the acts to overcome injustice on behalf of the victims of social and natural evils. Through such efforts we point toward the fulfillment of the kingdom.

The third type of sign is in history. We see the signs that point to the inadequacies of all other ideologies and systems to bring humanity to its ultimate fulfillment. We even acknowledge that the church in its human institutional form is so often partially or imperfectly the body of Christ. We persist in the hope and the promise that beyond history a state of existence is found in which the full blessings and glory of God are accomplished.

2. Signs of False Hopes. Not all signs of cosmic disorders point to the end of history. Repeatedly natural disasters have appeared. People have concluded that these were the signs of the end of the world. People have had hopes raised to high expectations that they would enjoy the physical return of Christ soon. When life returned to more normal circumstances and the Parousia had not occurred as they expected, they have become disillusioned. Jesus calls us to be awake, alert, and active through such disasters. They become occasion for giving signs of mercy and hope: signs of mercy by relief of the suffering disasters cause; signs of hope by the comfort to those who are bereaved.

Not all leaders who claim to read the signs of cosmic disorders and are certain that we are approaching the imminent end of time are true prophets. Indeed, Jesus warned that neither he nor the angels of God knew with certainty the day and the hour. That

23

should be enough of a caution to be wary of any who claim to have such knowledge. They may be claiming a superiority to Christ and should not be given full trust.

3. The Unchanging Word. Jesus said that God's words will never pass away. Some persons assume that all the words of scripture are identical with God's words. Obviously not every word of scripture is coterminous with God's words. Jesus himself pointed out instances in which words of the Old Testament needed interpretation. Some of the words of scripture are reports of what exists or has happened in history. They are not necessarily definitive for what God intends or requires.

It is Jesus who according to John is God's word embodied in human form. It is the kingdom that Jesus proclaimed which is God's full intention for humanity. Christians begin with Jesus Christ as the disclosure of God's unchanging word. Then we look for signs of opportunities to do the work of Christ in the midst of the changing vicissitudes of time. We look for signs that the kingdom of God is breaking into the midst of the change and align ourselves with God's unchanging word.

Illustrative Materials

1. Signs of the Fig Tree. God gives us constant signs of the persistence of life and goodness. Even in the midst of the greatest disasters we get signs of grace and mercy. After the disaster of the Russian earthquake of Neftegorsk Vladimir Chichin was pulled out after four days of being buried under the rubble. Workers had assumed that no one could any longer survive the devastation, lack of water, and cold temperatures. Doctors were even more amazed and considered it a miracle when a six-year-old boy and a two-month-old baby were pulled from the basement of an apartment house. They had been trapped for five nights in sub-freezing weather and yet survived with only scratches. The six-year-old boy kept his spirits up by singing and talking with others trapped around him.

We planted bushes along a bike trail on Earth Day. In the winter groundhogs chewed several of them off so that we had to dig through

24

mulch to see if anything was there. Some others appeared to be only dead sticks. All leaves and branches were gone. With the warmth of sun and spring rains suddenly leaves sprouted on what appeared to be dead sticks. Branches shot up from the midst of the mulch. In a couple weeks what appeared to be entirely gone had small branches five or six inches tall. Signs of summer and life were abundantly evident.

In the midst of a slum, in the cell of a prison, in an alcoholic bum, suddenly an amazing new life will emerge. A person will be aroused by the work of the Spirit. In a situation of seeming hopelessness a person will meet the warmth of God's mercy and the sun of righteousness and a life will turn around and bloom again.

2. Signs of God in History. The Communist regime in China tried to suppress the church. Church buildings were appropriated and used for storage, meetings or education. Christians who were known were exiled or sent to do manual labor. In 1995 the general secretary of the Three-Self Patriotic Movement said that China had 8 to 10 million Protestants, though some say it may be as many as 50 million. The China Christian Council said that three believers' groups start up about every two days. God gives signs of the Spirit's presence in the midst of persecution.

3. Reading Signs. Two fellows were traveling together on the Autobahn, the German superhighway. One of the fellows knew very little German. He turned to the other and remarked that they must be near a fairly large city he had never heard of before. He said the signs had been pointing to *Ausfahrt*. He did not know that *Ausfahrt* in German means exit! Are we, too, illiterate in the language of the Spirit so that we fail to read or misread God's signs for our lives?

4. Mistaken Signs. Hal Lindsey wrote a book called *The Late Great Planet Earth* (Grand Rapids, Michigan: Zondervan, 1970). He read as a sign of the approaching end times the establishment of Israel in 1948 as a return of the Jews after several centuries. He, along with others, thought that within 40 years, a generation in biblical calculations, the Parousia would occur. Did he misread the signs since it is more than 25 years since he published the warning and well over forty years since the establishment of Israel in Palestine and the Parousia has not yet occurred?

5. Descriptive vs. Prescriptive. Recently a group was discussing poverty in the United States. A few people dismissed the problem by quoting Jesus as saying you have the poor with you always. Others have quoted Jesus as saying that there will be wars and rumors of wars, and that those who take the sword shall die by the sword, as justification for participation in warfare. They argue that those who work for the elimination of warfare are wrong since Jesus predicted that these things would continue. They fail to distinguish words of scripture which are descriptive of what is as opposed to prescription for what should be. They do not give more weight to the scriptures' repeated admonitions to minister to the poor and the passages where Jesus, Paul, and John urge Christians to love one's enemies. They also ignore where Jesus calls Peter to put up his sword, which early Christians understood to mean that when Jesus disarmed Peter, he disarmed every Christian.

2. The One Shepherd

John 10:11-18

---

[11]"I am the good shepherd. The good shepherd lays down his life for the sheep. [12]The hired hand, who is not the shepherd and does not own the sheep, sees the wolf coming and leaves the sheep and runs away — and the wolf snatches them and scatters them. [13]The hired hand runs away because a hired hand does not care for the sheep. [14]I am the good shepherd. I know my own and my own know me, [15]just as the Father knows me and I know the Father. And I lay down my life for the sheep. [16]I have other sheep that do not belong to this fold. I must bring them also, and they will listen to my voice. So there will be one flock, one shepherd. [17]For this reason the Father loves me, because I lay down my life in order to take it up again. [18]No one takes it from me, but I lay it down of my own accord. I have power to lay it down, and I have power to take it up again. I have received this command from my Father."

Context

Context of the Church Year

The Good Shepherd parable comes on the fourth Sunday of Easter. While it is located in the Gospel before the crucifixion, it interprets the meaning of the events. The message enables the church to see them not as unrelenting tragedy and failure but as signs of victory and hope.

The key interpretation is not that the enemies of Jesus were in control by their ability to take his life. Rather it is that Jesus by an act of the will of God could lay down his life for his followers and take it up again. Their mission is to continue as his flock under his leadership as eternally present. They are to identify his other sheep and bring them into his flock.

The full meaning of the "I am the Good Shepherd" claim could not be understood by the disciples prior to Easter. At that time they could only think of it as pertaining to his earthly ministry. The extension of it into an unlimited future could only be understood by them and by us because of the Easter event. It is as they and we look back at it from beyond Easter that the full import of the claim becomes clear.

Context of the Lectionary

The First Lesson. (Acts 4:8-12) Even though Jesus was crucified the contention with his enemies continued. In this passage Peter asserts that the healings which the apostles performed were actually accomplished by the power of Jesus Christ, whom his enemies had had crucified but whom God had raised from the dead. Peter further made the bold claim that salvation, the fullest meaning of healing, was only possible according to the very being of Jesus Christ.

The Second Lesson. (1 John 3:16-24) The writer of 1 John picks up a theme from the parable of the Good Shepherd. He affirms that Jesus laid down his life for those who follow him. That places upon them the obligation to obey his commands, the primary one being the commandment to love. That love is defined in the final analysis by the example of Jesus, who served others to the extreme extent of giving his life willingly for them. His eternal presence enables his followers to obey the command to love in the same manner as he loved.

Gospel. (John 10:11-18) The parable of the Good Shepherd contains the statement by Jesus that an evidence that he is the shepherd is his readiness to lay down his life for the flock. Furthermore, he also has the power to take it up again. That sets him apart from the others who also acted in the past as shepherds when kings were also called shepherds.

Psalm. (Psalm 23) This Psalm of assurance was surely part of the basis for Jesus' claim to be the good shepherd. In light of the identification of the Lord as a shepherd, the claim to be the good shepherd lays claim to divinity on the part of Jesus. It is the resurrection which validates his claim.

The Context of the Gospel Lesson in John

We need to be aware that the parable of the Good Shepherd comes at the approaching climax of the conflict between Jesus and his detractors. The Gospel according to John develops the theme of increasing popularity of Jesus among the common people contrasted with increasing hostility from the leaders of the institutionalized religion of his day.

A central sign for Jesus, according to John, was the expulsion of the man born blind whom Jesus had healed (John 9). It was the growing and persistent acknowledging of Jesus as the Christ that led the man born blind to be expelled from the synagogue. Jesus then fully realized the depth of the opposition to his ministry and its impact on those who accepted him as the authentic agent of God, as the Messiah.

Jesus shifts the focus of his concern to a larger field. He is concerned for his disciples. But he is not limited to the small group close to him or to others who were ready to follow him because of his teaching and healing. He looked beyond with a larger vision to all those who stood in need of salvation.

Context of Related Scriptures

> Genesis 49:24 — Joseph's greatness supported by the Shepherd.
> Numbers 27:16-17 — Moses appoints a successor as a shepherd.
> Psalm 78:52-53 — Moses seen as a shepherd.

Isaiah 40:11 — The Suffering Servant as a shepherd.

Jeremiah 23:1-4 — The shepherds who scatter contrasted with the Lord who gathers the sheep and raises the shepherd.

Ezekiel 34 — Israel's false shepherds contrasted with God as the true shepherd.

Micah 2:12 — God's assurance that he will gather a remnant as sheep into a fold.

Matthew 10:16 — Disciples are sent like sheep amidst wolves.

Mark 14:27 — Jesus sees the disciples scattered like sheep when the shepherd is struck.

John 21:15-19 — The straying sheep return to the shepherd.

1 Peter 2:25 — The straying sheep return to the shepherd.

Content

Precis (John 10:11-18)

Jesus makes one of his "I am" claims. They appear frequently in the Gospel according to John. Jesus claims to be the good shepherd. He proceeds to define the good shepherd as one who lays down his life for the sheep. It is also implied that he is actually the owner of the sheep. The good shepherd who owns the sheep is contrasted with the hireling who, when he sees danger approaching, abandons the sheep and flees. When a shepherd flees in the face of dangers, some of the sheep are killed and the others are scattered.

Jesus proceeds to an analogy about the mutual knowledge between those who belong to him and his knowledge of them arising from the mutual knowledge between himself and God, referred to as the Father. He also extends the scope of his sheep beyond the disciples to whom the parable is addressed. He has other sheep as well. They are those who listen, with implications that they also obey and follow him.

Jesus concludes with an assertion of the voluntary nature of his death and his ability to recover his life. He makes the claim because he has been told to do so by God.

Thesis: The good shepherds are the ones who will readily lay down their life for the sheep.

Theme: Those who belong to Jesus are those who hear his teachings, obey them, and follow him.

Key Words in the Parable

1. "Good." (v. 11) The term indicates fitness for the task. It implies that Jesus is the model shepherd.

2. "Shepherd." (v. 11) A shepherd is one who cares for us by nourishing and protecting his sheep. He will do so even though it costs him his life. Therefore he can be trusted regardless of what happens.

3. "Hired Hand." (v. 12) The hireling only does the job because he is paid to do it, not because he really cares for the sheep. In the context of the time it referred to the leaders of Judaism who only took care of the people as long as they were paid to do the job and were not threatened by adversaries. From this, in part at least, the Quakers did not pay their leaders of meeting a fixed salary but only gave them gifts toward their support, for fear that they would become hirelings. They referred to the state church pastors as hirelings.

4. "Knows me, know the Father." (v. 15) For Jesus, God was not an abstract being or an intellectual concept. The knowledge of each for the other arises from an I-Thou relationship of personal interaction. It was not merely an I-It relationship. It was also a tenderly mutual affair.

5. "Other Sheep." (v. 16) In the claim of Jesus to have other sheep Paul and others found authorization to include Gentiles in the church. The criteria for inclusion is not genealogy but the readiness to accept the lordship of Jesus.

6. "Fold; Flock." (v. 16) The term *fold* tends to put the emphasis on the place. The term *flock* shifts the emphasis to the persons. It is not where the sheep are, such as in Israel, but who they are, that is, obedient followers of Jesus.

Contemplation

Issues and Insights

1. The Divinity of Jesus. The so-called "I am" passages of John are assertions supporting the claim that Jesus was of divine nature in a special way. In this parable or extended metaphor John is asserting the basis of Jesus' divinity as arising from a special relationship. He was intimate with God as a son to a father.

Jesus not only had perfect knowledge of the Father so that he had a kind of intellectual unity with him. He also was in perfect obedience to the will of God. Ultimately it is God who is the giver of life. Jesus was ready to let that life be taken away in obedience to his mission as the Christ. Because he was fully aware of God's power over life he believed that he could receive it again.

2. The Call to Belong to Jesus. If we claim to be Christian it places a special demand upon us. We are to enter into the same kind of personal relationship with Jesus that he had with the Father. It means that we know fully his intentions and his will so that we partake of his nature in ourselves.

The demand is not to know a set of propositions or a list of rules to follow. We do not live according to the law. It is rather to know a person so completely that our will is in unity with his. In that sense we also partake of a measure of divinity. We have given our life into his hands because we trust that only through him do we have the power to give up our life and receive it back again. Then we experience life in its fullest realization.

3. Self-Sacrificing. The first law of life for those who do not trust their life to the power of God is to preserve their life. Any measure is justified to maintain their life. They are like the hired hands who ask that they perform only so long as they are paid for doing the job and can save their own skin.

Jesus calls his followers to be shepherds rather than sheep and good shepherds in the sense that he was. We are to care enough for people that we are ready to let our life be taken rather than abandon them. So sacrificial living for others is the first law of life. It is not in preserving our life at all costs that we are followers of Jesus. It is our readiness to let it be taken in obedience to God's will that we receive life in its fullest.

4. Who are the Wolves, Robbers and Thieves? The early church lived in the midst of persecution. The passage about the danger to the sheep from attack was very real to them. That was especially the case in the time when the leaders of the church were specifically targeted for persecution in the attempt to eliminate Christianity. They knew who their adversaries were. To have the message that the good shepherds were those who gave their life for the sheep rather than abandon them was a great strength and comfort.

Most western Christians live in situations where they are seldom threatened with loss of life for being Christian. The dangers are more subtle but just as real. They come from threats to our readiness to follow Jesus completely. The threats are in the false values that are propagated as giving the real meaning to life. We are assailed with the notion that serving self, that striving for comfort, that avoiding even the slightest pain or suffering is what life is about.

Any threat to our standard of living is offered as the wolves, robbers and thieves. Thus an illegal immigrant is a person to be rejected. A person of another race or ethnic group is to be hated. So we are to fight any relinquishing of our national interest or sovereignty for the welfare of the larger global society so that other people who are in dire straits may have a better life. Any question about our status as number one in the world requires that we spend more for sophisticated weapons and a stronger armed force to enhance our security.

Are not these the assumptions and values that enter into the fold and scatter the flock today?

5. The Role of Leadership. Two differing styles of leadership can be observed. One is to exercise power and dominion over people. It uses force to make people do what they don't want to do. It seeks power and benefits for self-aggrandizement. Such leadership generates resentment and hatred. It usually ends up hurting people and causing injustice. Such leaders drive people from behind with threats and punishment. It tends toward tyranny.

Another type of leadership is the shepherd-servant style. It assumes the burdens of people. It demonstrates by a life lived at a level above the flock what should be done to achieve higher purposes. It relieves the hurts and pains of the followers. It invites people to follow because they want to do so rather than forcing them by fear and threat.

Jesus as the suffering servant and the good shepherd provides a model for Christian leadership.

Homily Hints

1. The Good Shepherd. (v. 11) The sermon could deal with how Jesus exemplified the Good Shepherd.
    A. How Jesus Related to His Disciples
        1. Inviting to follow
        2. Teaching and supporting
    B. How Jesus Related to Those Outside the Flock
        1. Healing the Syro-Phoenician woman
        2. Forgiving the tax collectors
        3. Healing the Roman nobleman's child
    C. How Jesus Related to God
        1. Perfect understanding of God's will
        2. Obedience even unto death on the cross

2. I Know the Father. (v. 15) Examine the issue of how we know the Father.
    A. Through the Life of Jesus
    B. Through Others who Know God
    C. By Cultivating the Presence of the Holy Spirit

3. One Flock, One Shepherd. (v. 16) What is the ecumenical vision? How do we relate to Christians of other traditions? What is the nature of Christian unity?

A. Openness to listen to the beliefs and needs of others
B. Ready to testify to the truth we hold firmly
C. Humility about the certainty of our position; ready to listen to firmly-held beliefs of others
D. Separation only when others reject us and our position

4. Heed My Voice. (v. 16) How can we heed the voice of Jesus speaking to us today?

A. Steep Oneself in Scripture about Jesus
B. Be Sensitive to the Hurts and Pains of People
C. Seek to be Faithful to Jesus' command in Word and Deed

5. The Sheep Are His Own. (v. 14) The importance of the Christian community to identify itself as the Body of Christ.

A. The Community Forgiven and Being Forgiven by Christ
B. The Community Carrying forward Jesus' Ministry of Teaching, Preaching, and Healing
C. The Community Inviting Others to Come into the Fold

6. Validating Belief. (vv. 11-18) Jesus says he is the Good Shepherd because he is willing to go to the extreme measure of giving his life for his sheep.

A. Validated by Obedience to Christ — even under persecution and threat
B. Validated in Upholding And Protecting Others — tending to the welfare of the neighbor
C. Validated by the Test of Love — even for the enemy

Contact

Points of Contact

Vulnerability. People are very vulnerable. A television ad points out the fragility of life. It points out that persons can only

35

live two or three months without food, a few days without water and only a few minutes without air. It then asks how long a person can live without love. The image of the shepherd is of one who cares for the sheep, a particularly vulnerable animal. Contrary to other animals which have sharp teeth or fangs, claws with talons, or other means for aggression or defense, a sheep has very little in the way of means for inflicting injury on another or defending itself. They need a shepherd to care for them.

People need to know that at the heart of the universe there is care for the person. Jesus' identification of himself as a shepherd points to a God who is compassionate and caring. Persons often fall short of their own self-image. They know that they have not lived up to the best that is in them. If God is harsh, judgmental, and condemnatory, people will fear him. If God is characterized more as a caring shepherd, they can know that despite their failures and tendency to stray from being their best they can still be accepted and try anew.

One of the strongest reasons for opposition to Jesus was his claim to forgive sins. The good shepherd extends hope of forgiveness to vulnerable people. They receive his care and compassion. The good pastor (the Latin word for shepherd) will extend that kind of caring and support to people aware of their failures and vulnerability.

A Global Mission. Two concerns may be addressed from this passage. They deal with Jesus' statement that he has other sheep not of this fold. The disciples understood from this statement that it was for them to gather the persons who were outside the fold. That gave the impulse for missions. In a culture that values diversity and pluralism the issue of evangelism and missions is one which needs new consideration and vision.

The so-called "white man's burden" for inferior cultures and more primitive people no longer gives impetus for missions. Many of the cultures which are not heavily influenced by Christianity are quite sophisticated today. The level of culture in a country such as Japan is quite advanced. The people generally enjoy a high standard of living and longevity of life. Do they still need to be brought to Christianity to know the fullness of life? Is it enough that they are adjusted and satisfied with their religious understandings? The mission work of many denominations is suffering today because church members no longer feel the same impulse for missions that they did a century ago.

The same question can be raised about how you evangelize in a culture and society that wants to emphasize the value of diversity. The melting pot image is no longer the dominant one in American society. Perhaps the image of the variegated colors of a patchwork quilt is the dominant one.

Only as we experience the joys and security of the Christian life can we invite other persons to join us in the fold, to come to Christ and his church. It is not necessary to put down the values that people already have in order to engage in evangelism and missions. It is rather to offer to them even more and greater values in the personal knowledge of Christ's compassion and love that offers to people an even fuller meaning and experience of what life should be.

Illustrative Materials

1. Laying Down Life for Others. Raoul Wallenberg, a Lutheran, was a Swedish diplomat in World War II. He used his post in Hungary to aid 30,000 Jews to escape persecution and death from the Nazi party. Just before the Soviet Union invaded Budapest, he persuaded the Nazi officials not to execute 70,000 other Jews and so saved their lives. He was captured by the Russians, who claimed he was a spy for the Americans. He almost certainly suffered death himself in a Soviet prison. What happened to him and why he suffered from the Soviets rather than from the Nazis is not clear. It is, however, clear that he was a good shepherd who gave his life for people who were different from him religiously and who were the object of hatred, fear, and destruction by others.

2. Hirelings, Robbers and Wolves. A number of television evangelists have been exposed recently as betraying their office as a shepherd or pastor. Jim Bakker engaged in a scheme which essentially defrauded many people who thought they were investing in security for their old age with a Christian organization. His downfall came when he let his sexual desires consume him.

Others have disclosed that their interest was really for serving their own needs rather than the flock which they gathered through their radio and television ministries. They served their own needs with lavish living and immorality while they presented themselves as pastors concerned for others.

3. Giving Life For Other Sheep. Corrie ten Boom tells the story of her family's efforts to save Jews from the Holocaust during World War II in the Netherlands. (*The Hiding Place*, by Corrie ten Boom with John and Elizabeth Sherrill. Carmel, New York: Guideposts Associates, Inc., 1971.) She and her family, who were Dutch Reformed Christians, worked through much of the war at great risk to themselves to hide Jews. Eventually they were discovered, arrested and sent to concentration camps. Corrie ten Boom survived after much suffering to tell the story, but her father and sister both died in the camps, giving up their lives in the attempt to save others.

3. The Fruitful Vine

John 15:1-8

---

¹ "I am the true vine, and my Father is the vinegrower. ²He removes every branch in me that bears no fruit. Every branch that bears fruit he prunes to make it bear more fruit. ³You have already been cleansed by the word that I have spoken to you. ⁴Abide in me as I abide in you. Just as the branch cannot bear fruit by itself unless it abides in the vine, neither can you unless you abide in me. ⁵I am the vine, you are the branches. Those who abide in me and I in them bear much fruit, because apart from me you can do nothing. ⁶Whoever does not abide in me is thrown away like a branch and withers; such branches are gathered, thrown into the fire, and burned. ⁷If you abide in me, and my words abide in you, ask for whatever you wish, and it will be done for you. ⁸My Father is glorified by this, that you bear much fruit and become my disciples."

What is a preacher to make of a parable or extended allegory about a vine in an urban and industrial culture? If you are living in a small town or a rural area, people might know something about growing grapes. They might know about the need to prune back old growth since the grapes only form on the new growth. But how many in a large city would know about cultivating a grape vine so that it produces a good crop? For them grapes are something you buy in the produce section of the supermarket.

Perhaps a more meaningful allegory might relate to electricity. After all, most of us are heavily dependent upon electrical current. We know that electricity is generated somewhere else. It has to be transmitted over an extensive network of lines to reach us. We can tap into it by plugging various devices into outlets and the current can produce light or heat or run various kinds of motors. It can even operate computers, radios, televisions, telephones and other devices that allow us to communicate with others or they to communicate with us. If we turn off the switch or a fuse is blown, we lose the power.

For most of us all this happens in some mysterious way that we do not fully understand. We take it for granted until something causes the electricity to fail. Then we are left in the dark, are cold, cannot cook, worry about things defrosting and spoiling, and have a kind of silence as telephone, television, radio and computer go dead.

Still, something is lacking in the allegory of electricity. It does not have the organic nature of a grape vine. It is mechanical. It does not have the same connection with life that the vine has. We are even rather uneasy about the suggestion that a computer that operates on electrical switches and magnetic memory is somewhat akin to the mind and has a capacity for "artificial intelligence."

So we probably go back to the allegory of the vine and try to make it understandable to a culture that is not agricultural. We are dealing with life and not some mechanical operation.

Context

Context of the Season

This Sunday is part of the season following Easter and before Pentecost. We are treating the implications of the crucifixion and resurrection. The passage for this Sunday is part of the preparation Jesus made for his disciples prior to his crucifixion but in anticipation of it. The disciples needed to be ready for the time when he would no longer be present in the flesh.

We, too, live without the physical presence of Jesus. We still need to relate to the spiritual presence of the resurrected Christ. After participating in the high days of Good Friday and Easter, people have a tendency to be let down. They need to be uplifted and reminded of the importance of continued abiding in Christ in the ongoing work with him beyond the celebrative occasions of the church year.

Context of the Lectionary

The First Lesson. (Acts 8:26-40) The passage relates the ministry of Philip and his encounter with the Ethiopian Eunuch. Philip was directed to travel the wilderness road from Jerusalem to Gaza. As he went he met the court official, who was reading the prophet Isaiah and was puzzled by the text about the sheep led to the slaughter. Philip was able to interpret it for him in the light of the recent crucifixion and resurrection of Jesus. He enlarged upon it to tell him all the good news about Jesus. That led the Ethiopian to ask to be baptized, which Philip proceeded to do. The Ethiopian went on his way rejoicing.

The Second Lesson. (1 John 4:7-21) John asserts that God is love and all that means for love of brothers and sisters. God's love is manifested in the sending of his Son who was sacrificed out of love to atone for our sins. In response to that great love, we should abide in him and thereby manifest the same kind of love. He concludes the section with the observation that you cannot claim to love God if you hate your brothers and sisters.

Gospel. (John 15:1-8) The claim is one of the "I am" statements John attributes to Jesus. Jesus is the vine and the Father is the vinedresser. The image is further developed by suggesting that the disciples are the fruit of the vine if they stay connected to Jesus and produce works which demonstrate that connection.

Psalm. (Psalm 22:25-31) The emphasis of the Psalm is on the praise of the Lord. It is an affirmation of the trust that he will care for the poor and that he has dominion over life and death. That confidence extends unto future generations who will experience his deliverance.

Context of Related Scriptures

Psalm 80:8-19 — God transplants a vine from Egypt to plant it and tend it elsewhere.

41

Isaiah 5:1-7 — A love song concerning the vineyard.

Jeremiah 2:21 — A lament that the good transplanted vine became a wild one.

Ezekiel 15:1-6 — A judgment on the dead vine in the midst of the woods.

Ezekiel 19:10-14 — The image of a vine that has been subjected to fire.

Hosea 10:1 — Israel is compared to a luxuriant vine.

Matthew 21:28-41 — Two parables about the vineyard.

Galatians 5:22 — The fruits of the Spirit.

Content

Precis (John 15:1-8)

Jesus identifies himself as the vine and the vinegrower as the Father. He presses the analogy in several respects: the vinegrower removes the unfruitful branches; he prunes the branches to make them bear more fruit; the branches need to be attached to the vine and draw sustenance from them to bear fruit; and the unfruitful branches are eventually cut off, gathered and burned.

Jesus ends by an admonition to the disciples to abide in him and to bear appropriate fruit. In so doing they give God the honor due.

Thesis: Christ is the source of spiritual life and fruit for his disciples.

Theme: Abiding in the life and teachings of Christ is the source of the Christian's good works.

Key Words in the Parable

1. "I am." (v. 1) John repeatedly makes claims for the person of Jesus by using "I am" statements. He uses symbols of ordinary life-giving or life-protecting things such as water, bread, a shepherd and light to try to point beyond themselves to the greater

42

being of Jesus. Because Jesus was so qualitatively different from other persons, he had to be described in these various ways to try to communicate his full grandeur.

2. "The True Vine." (v. 1) Usually the symbols chosen in the "I am" statements were qualified by some adjective that indicated Jesus' greatness beyond the symbol itself; thus it was "living" water, "good" shepherd and "true" vine. The symbol of the vine may have resulted from a double occurrence that night: they had drunk of the fruit of the vine at the supper in the upper room; the experience in Gethsamene, with its vineyards nearby, lay just ahead of them.

3. "The Vinegrower." (v. 1) The Old Testament frequently alluded to God as the vinegrower. Jesus had used parables of the vineyard with God represented as the vinegrower earlier in his teachings. The growing of grapes was a significant part of the Palestinian economy. A good or bad crop could make a substantial difference for the well-being of the society, especially where people generally lived on the margin. Careless vinegrowers who did not care well for the crop could affect the livelihood of many. In a like manner God watched over and cared for the livelihood of his people.

4. "Removes Every Branch." (v. 2) Any branch of a vine that does not bear fruit draws nourishment away from those that do. If they are permitted to remain on the vine, the crop will be smaller and of less quality. So a good vinedresser will remove the non-bearing branches.

5. "He Prunes." (v. 2) Pruning is necessary to force the vine to produce new growth. It is on the new growth that fruit develops. The more new growth, the greater the harvest.

6. "Already Cleansed." (v. 3) The allusion here is probably twofold. In chapter 13 John had told of the footwashing and the rebuke of Peter when he wanted to be washed all over (vv. 9, 10). In the following verse (v. 11) Jesus referred to the exclusion of

Judas as a part of the cleansing process. This represents a bit of mixing of the metaphor, though cutting off the dead branches and pruning the fruit-bearing branches was a type of cleansing. A word play is found in Greek between "pruning" (*airei*) and "cleaning" (*cathairei*).

7. "The Word." (v. 3) The word is not simply the letters on a page or the sound of a voice. It is produced by the breath, which is the same word in Greek and Hebrew as spirit. A spoken word carried with it the breath or life force of the person who said it. Jesus spoke with the authority of his person and thus carried with it the cleansing of forgiveness.

8. "Abide in me." (vv. 4, 5, 7) Persons who are in harmony with each other receive mutual strength. John has a mystical sense of life force flowing between persons. Where the disciples were in unity of thought and purpose with Jesus, they partook of the same energy for life that he received from the Father.

9. "Glorified." (v. 8) The Father is honored when additional disciples are won to obedience to God's commands and they bear fruit. That is the purpose of the vine being attached to the branches. It is a foreshadowing of the mandate given after the resurrection to the disciples in Matthew 28:18, 19 and to Peter in John 21:15-17.

Contemplation

Issues and Insights

1. Unity in Diversity. The image of the vine suggests a unity in diversity. The vine has roots that give rise to the stock. From the stock, branches develop. The branch puts forth shoots. From the shoots come the multiplicity of leaves and grapes. They show forth a diversity and yet are so connected that the parts relate to each other to form a living plant.

In like manner the church shows a diversity of parts but a connectedness that gives it a wholeness in organic unity. It becomes a

44

living body when it is connected to God through Christ. The Holy Spirit energizes the church as it flows through the lives of the members. The church in its various branches brings forth a multiplicity of fruits from its differing members.

2. Love and Obedience. The vine is used as a symbol of connectedness. Jesus calls upon his disciples to live according to the command of love. Such a love is more than an emotional feeling of liking someone. It moves back and forth in such a way that it works for the welfare of all the members and thus seeks the welfare of the whole. It is more a matter of the will and intent to act than it is of a sentiment or emotion.

To God in Christ mutual love in the church represents a response of gratitude for the way his love is given for us. That gratitude is also more than a sentiment. It is a desire and a willingness to be like Christ, to have him control our life. We then become his emissaries, reaching out to others with concern for their welfare, as Christ has expressed his toward us. That leads us to obedience to God's commands as given to us by Jesus Christ. We know that it is in obedience to God's intents and purposes that we realize our highest welfare, and that is true for others as well. So we invite them to the same goodness of life which we enjoy.

3. Fruit: Cause or Effect? It is not our fruit, our works that connect us to the vine. It is because we are connected to the vine that we are able to produce fruit. The old argument of faith or works is resolved in the image of the vine. We do not come to salvation because of our works. We come to salvation because of God's action and our response of trust and faith in Christ.

Nevertheless, we cannot say that we have known the saving grace of Christ unless it produces fruit. It must produce the works of righteousness or we are not truly connected to him as living branches are connected to the vine. If we fail to bring forth the fruits because of the life of Christ flowing into us through the activity of the Holy Spirit, we are as dead wood that is to be discarded.

4. Pruning the Vine. The church has usually found discipline a difficult problem. This parable with its image of the pruning of the vine and the cutting away of dead branches suggests the need for some discipline. The issue is not whether discipline is needed, but who exercises it, how it is done, and for what end.

It is clear that with the help of the Holy Spirit and the teachings and example of Jesus Christ we need to cut out of our lives that which prevents us from living according to the commands of God. All of us come into fellowship with Christ with sins in our being. We constantly struggle with our weaknesses and failures despite our best intentions and strongest efforts. Our resolve to be faithful in following Christ needs to be renewed and upheld constantly. As someone has said, the church is composed of persons who are forgiven sinners who are also sinners needing to be forgiven.

The harder questions are whether the corporate body exercises some kind of discipline over us and how. It seems clear from the teachings and examples of the New Testament that discipline should be for redemption and not as punishment or vengeance. It always needs to be tempered with compassion for the person enmeshed in sin. Too often in church history that was lost from sight. Such legal fictions as turning over to the state for punishment those who were to be disciplined were used. It at least recognized that the church should be redemptive and not punitive.

Some congregations have acknowledged that some persons no longer show by their actions in producing fruits that they are committed to that particular manifestation of the Body of Christ. After repeated attempts to renew the relationship or urging such members to join another congregation where they would be in active fellowship, they remove the members from the roll of the congregation. The congregation does not thereby pass final judgment as to whether the person is still a Christian. It does try to let the persons know their true condition. The members have shown by their inactivity and lack of connectedness that they are no longer in living fellowship with that congregation.

5. Abiding in Christ. If a vine is cut off from the source in its root, it dies. Likewise the new life in Christ withers and dies unless it is continuously nourished by drawing on the source of life. The fellowship with Christ needs to be renewed regularly. That needs to be done in a variety of ways.

One way to renew the spirit is by participating in the worship of the church. Through the reminders in the public reading of scripture, in corporate prayer, in the rituals which are done in remembrance of what Christ has done, and in the living word proclaimed by a living messenger, a person is brought back into contact with the source and can be again renewed.

Perhaps even more important is a regular practice of prayer, study of the scripture, meditation on the person of Christ, and reflection on what the will of God calls us to do each day. It also means acknowledging our failures, accepting forgiveness, and through gratitude for the opportunity for new beginnings to seek to be more faithful in producing good fruits.

A further way to stay in contact with the source of Christian life is to look upon each person with whom we relate and to try to see him as Christ would see him. We look at him not in our self-righteousness, but asking, "What do I see of Christ in this person potentially? How can I help him to come to the fullness of Christ by the way I relate to this person?"

Homily Hints

1. The Vine and the Branches. (vv. 1-8) The sermon could go one of two directions: the unity of a church despite differences among persons, between congregations, or even between denominations; or it might discuss the variety of gifts needed by the Body of Christ.
   A. The God of Diversity
   B. The Contributions of Differences
   C. The Organic Nature of Our Unity

2. Pruning and Cleansing. (v. 2) The need we have to examine ourselves constantly and to cut away that which is dead wood.
   A. Cutting away the Evil
   B. Restricting Wants and Desires
   C. Filling Life with Positive Good

3. Abiding in Christ. (vv. 4-6) Review the issue of how persons can draw strength and grow by fellowship with Christ. What are the resources and techniques for receiving the Holy Spirit's presence?

    A. Productive Prayer Life — Includes waiting for Christ to speak to our condition and the Holy Spirit to empower us to do as he directs.

    B. Searching the Scriptures — Using them to help know the person and message of Christ.

    C. Exercising Obedience — As the body is strengthened by exercise, so the spirit develops strength by consciously ordering behavior to concur with the commands and examples of Jesus.

    D. Fellowship of Believers — Using the support, encouragement and discernment of other Christians to bring us to fellowship with Christ.

4. Discipleship and Fruitbearing. (vv. 2, 4, 5, 8) If we receive the forgiving and renewing power of Christ, we should bear the fruits and give evidence of it.

    A. The Fruits of Witnessing

    B. The Fruits of Ethical Action

    C. The Fruits of Good Works

    D. The Fruits of the Beloved Community

5. How to Glorify God. (v. 8) What in the Christian life gives honor and respect to God? How does our life show the God whom we worship?

    A. Loving Fellow Christians — Mutual Welfare

    B. Loving Our Neighbors — The Welfare of Outsiders

    C. Loving Our Enemies — The Ultimate Test of Love

    D. Winning Others to God — The Evangelistic Impulse

Contact

Points of Contact

1. Dependence to Interdependence. Persons are not isolated individuals. We are born almost entirely dependent upon others to survive and grow to maturity. We never become entirely independent. We always need at least other life to give us life. Even the hermit or recluse has to have food that comes from other life forms. The mature individuals are the persons who have the capacity to give life to others through their life.

In the life of the Spirit we need to be nourished by the Holy Spirit to give newness and maturity to others. We move from dependence for the new birth to where we have the capacity to help others come to newness of life by inviting them to come to Christ as the source of the life of the spirit. We become interdependent when we receive from outside ourselves the nurture that we need, but we also give so that others can also grow spiritually.

2. Fruitful Service. Everyone wants life to be meaningful and significant. Persons often feel that their life counts for very little or that they have little power or not much to contribute. When they can identify with the Kingdom of God and the glory of God's work, they can realize their own significance as part of the larger scheme of things.

The fruits of the spirit are not necessarily measured by the standards of success that the world around us uses. The fruits of the spirit are measured by the degree of our faithfulness in following Christ. To the world in general that may not appear as significant, but if we believe and trust that Christ really shows us the full meaning of life and history, then such trust and obedience is of the most significance.

We speak of having a worship service. Even true worship in which we commit our lives to honoring God and acting in accord with God's will for our lives is an act of fruitful service. It will then lead us into other acts of fruitful service outside of the formal worship services.

3. Character and Personality. Character is formed and personality develops according to the goals and purposes of life. If we have as our goal to grow in Christ-likeness, in the image of God that we have seen in Jesus, then our acts in moving toward that goal will change our character and form our personality.

One of the characteristics that distinguishes human personhood from other animals is our ability to choose and shape our own destiny. Abiding in Christ is a choice that is built-in for the Christian. It is the recognition that Jesus Christ is the apex of development of character and personality. To dedicate life to openness to his spirit and the transformation of our life becomes a life-shaping activity.

4. Ridding Life of Obstacles to Growth. Temptation to do what we know we should not is a common human experience. At times our natural impulses and desires tend to take over and direct our actions. They may be as mild as the temptation to take those extra calories. They may be as extreme as the hate for someone sufficient to want to injure or kill him. They may even drive one to such despair that we want to take our own life.

It is very difficult to prune away these impulses or desires by our own resolve alone. It is not enough just to say "no" to them. The most effective way of ridding our lives from these obstacles to spiritual growth is to replace the impulses and desires with an alternative and positive impulse or desire. Abiding in Christ may give hope instead of despair. Trying to work for the welfare of others because of Christ's love for them may turn hate into love. Hungering for the approval of Christ and for righteousness may replace hunger for those calories.

Psychologists tell us that feelings are likely to follow our actions. So if we act as Christ would act even when we don't feel like it, and thus abide in him, our feelings toward others and ourselves are likely to conform to Christ's commands.

5. The Consequences Lead to Joy. Some would emphasize the dread of the fire that burns the dead branches. The joy in Christ and the glorification of God does not come from the motive of fear.

Joy comes from the awareness of approval of God in Christ. It comes from awareness of being in fellowship and under the care of a loving God. It comes from the awareness that our life is empowered and directed by the very source and meaning of life itself. It comes not so much because of what we do, but who we are as persons connected to God in Christ.

50

1. Abiding and Acting. Two major figures in church history demonstrate the results of meditation and devotion to Christ, abiding in him.

A. Bernard of Clairvaux was a monk who was part of the movement of the Medieval period that tried to achieve a mystical union with God. He is noted for his steps to mystical union which he composed. The story is told that he was riding a donkey along beautiful Lake Geneva. Anyone who has been there knows the magnificent scenery that surrounds it. That evening at supper he raised the query as to whether they had passed some body of water during the day. He was so engrossed in his meditation that he was scarcely aware of the grandeur around him!

Too often we tend to think of such persons as detached and not very active. That was not true of Bernard. He was amazingly productive. He founded the monastery at Clairvaux in eastern France. From there monasteries were founded under his guidance in eight other countries. He carried on a voluminous correspondence with all these countries. He was a counselor to kings and several popes. He may in fact have been the most powerful person in Europe at the time. He was also very productive in writing.

B. John Wesley is known for his piety and the holiness movement that arose from his life. The name Methodist comes from a club which his brother Charles started at Oxford and which John joined. It was a life of methodical prayer and scripture study. John pursued such contemplation throughout his life.

Again, he was amazingly productive and active. He preached two to four times every day, preaching more than 40,000 sermons in his lifetime. He traveled 4500 miles per year carrying his message throughout the country, most of it by horseback. He also visited Ireland and Scotland many times and went twice to the Netherlands.

2. Techniques for Abiding.

A. Brother Lawrence was a monk who was known for practicing the presence of God. He tried to be aware of God no matter what he was doing. Even while he was cooking he would carry on an internal conversation with God. His life and character have been an inspiration to countless others because of this simple way of trying always to know Christ was present with him in everything he did.

B. Frank Laubach is widely known for starting a literacy movement. The motto that he used to spread teaching to read was "Each One Teach One."

He may be less known for his "Game of Minutes." He tried to bring back into consciousness each minute that God was speaking to him and directing him. When speaking to groups, he would at times pause, look up and, talking to himself, say, "Thank you, God, for giving me that thought. I had not thought of it before." That was not self-righteous posing but was a result of his "Game of Minutes."

3. Different Fruits. Some wonder if Christians should produce fruits of evangelism or social action. That is a false choice. If we use the analogy of the vine, we know that different kinds of grapes come from different vines. My wife noted that green and red grapes were on sale at a local supermarket. She asked me to buy a bunch. When I got there and saw they were the same price, I could not decide which to buy so I bought some of each! They were both delicious.

In the '60s we lived in a house that had been owned by an avid gardener. On our lot we had a tree to which he had grafted two additional branches. The tree produced two kinds of apples and one of pears. All of them were good fruits.

4. Effects of Pruning. In the new property that a couple bought they had a small grape vine area. The first year they had such a harvest that the wife felt it was more than they needed. She did try to preserve all of the grapes by making grape juice and jelly.

The second year she felt it was too much to harvest and process so she gave many of the grapes away to neighbors and friends. The third year they did not want that many grapes. So in the spring she proceeded to cut back the vines radically, presuming that they would not produce as much. Instead the vines had new growth and the harvest was even more abundant than before.

5. Why Prune? Not only vines but also other fruit trees need to be pruned. The secret of pruning is to cut back excess growth so that the sap can give life to new growth where fruit develops. The pruning should also let in as much sunlight as possible so that the leaves can store the energy of the sun. The pruning needs to allow space for the fruit to mature. If you want large fruit such as peaches, pears or apples, you should also thin out the fruit so that more of the nourishment goes into those that are left.

4. Tying Up A Strong Man

Mark 3:20-35

20And the crowd came together again, so that they could not even eat. 21When his family heard it, they went out to restrain him, for people were saying, "He has gone out of his mind." 22And the scribes who came down from Jerusalem said, "He has Beelzebul, and by the ruler of the demons he casts out demons." 23And he called them to him, and spoke to them in parables, "How can Satan cast out Satan? 24If a kingdom is divided against itself, that kingdom cannot stand. 25And if a house is divided against itself, that house will not be able to stand. 26And if Satan has risen up against himself and is divided, he cannot stand, but his end has come. 27But no one can enter a strong man's house and plunder his property without first tying up the strong man; then indeed the house can be plundered.

28"Truly I tell you, people will be forgiven for their sins and whatever blasphemies they utter; 29but whoever blasphemes against the Holy Spirit can never have forgiveness, but is guilty of an eternal sin" —30for they had said, "He has an unclean spirit."

31Then his mother and his brothers came; and standing outside, they sent to him and called him. 32A crowd was sitting around him; and they said to him, "Your mother and your brothers and sisters are outside, asking for you." 33And he replied, "Who are my mother and my brothers?" 34And looking at those who sat around him, he said, "Here are my mother and my brothers! 35Whoever does the will of God is my brother and sister and mother."

Mark's gospel account very quickly gets into the conflict that will eventually culminate in the death of Jesus. Despite, or because of, Jesus' works which aroused wonder and amazement in the multitudes, opposition also arose. Any activity so extraordinary upset the status quo. His popularity threatened the authority and leadership of the official religion. They had to try to put it down before it got out of hand. Even the friends and family of Jesus were concerned about him.

How often do people try to restrict and constrain anyone who breaks with conventional ideas and practice? They like people to be religious in comfortable and conventional ways. They become alarmed or distressed if someone goes overboard and tries to live out religious commitment too fully or too radically.

But a real issue is raised by the fine line that sometimes separates the true religious proclamation and the claims of a person who is a fanatic. When is such a person really shaking us up to arouse us out of our complacency in accepting the familiar evil? Or when is the person stepping across the bounds of sanity into the unreal world of fantasy? How much do you tolerate the apparently aberrant behavior to test whether it is true or false? How do you protect against gullibility in following a leader because of the intensity of conviction while risking that you may be missing a true messenger from God?

The passage from Mark raises some disturbing questions. It challenges us to ask which party we would belong to in the controversy over the person of Jesus and his call for us to follow him today.

Context

Context of the Season

We have moved beyond the high holy days of Good Friday, Easter, and Pentecost. We are in the longest period of the church year when the agenda is not set by pointing toward a major event. More latitude is given but also less direction for choice or what to emphasize.

In this time of the church year the preacher has more choice and therefore more responsibility to consider what the needs of a specific congregation are. It is an opportune time to assess where people are and to try to pinpoint needs. The message can be more directly intended to emphasize themes that have been neglected or overlooked.

Context of the Gospel

Up to this point Mark reports the beginnings of Jesus' ministry. He did a number of remarkable healings. These had stirred the interest of many persons. He had begun to gather a following. Immediately preceding the section for today, Jesus had selected twelve out of those who showed an interest in his ministry.

Not much controversy had arisen so far. Jesus had responded to a question about fasting, since he did not follow the practices of the Pharisees and the followers of John the Baptist. His answer, with implicit claims about his understanding of the era they were experiencing, would have raised eyebrows at the least. Even more disturbing was his teaching and practice about the Sabbath. That was a more direct challenge to established religion of the day.

The two issues of fasting and sabbath observance plus his rising popularity reached all the way from Galilee to Jerusalem. According to Mark that set the stage for a more official confrontation between Jesus and official religious authorities.

Context of the Lectionary

The First Lesson. (1 Samuel 8:4-11, 16-20) Facing the constant threat from the highly organized Philistines, the people of Israel wanted Samuel to appoint a king. At first Samuel refused and pointed to the various unhappy consequences of having a king to rule over them. Despite his warnings about the tyranny of a king, the people persisted in having a government like that of other nations.

The Second Lesson. (2 Corinthians 4:13—5:1) Paul, in writing to the church at Corinth, reaffirms his belief that the God who raised Jesus from the dead would also grant them a similar outcome. They are encouraged not to lose heart and to maintain hope that their brief affliction would be rewarded with eternal life in the presence of God.

Gospel. (Mark 3:20-35) Jesus has his first encounter with a delegation of scribes from Jerusalem. They challenged his work of casting out demons and proposed that he could do it because he was in league with the ruler of the demons. Jesus turns the argument around and argues instead that he is able to heal exactly because he has defeated the ruler of demons. Jesus also has to resist pressures of friends and family who want him to desist from his public ministry because they think he is on the verge of going crazy.

Psalm. (Psalm 138) The Psalm begins with an expression of thanks to the Lord because of strength given. The psalmist looks forward to the time when all the kings will praise the Lord. The final section of the Psalm is an affirmation of faith that God will preserve him against all enemies and in the midst of troubles.

Context of Related Scriptures

Parallel passages are found in Matthew 12:22-32 and Luke 11:14-23. It could be instructive to note similarities and differences among the three accounts.

> 2 Kings 1:2-4 — Ahaziah wants a consultation with Baalzebub after an injury from a fall.
>
> Matthew 25:31-46 — The division between the sheep and the goats.
>
> Acts 26:24 — Festus thinks Paul is out of his mind and insane.
>
> 2 Corinthians 5:13 — Paul says that if he is beside himself, it is for God; if we are in our right mind it is for you.
>
> John 10:19-21 — A division arose where some contended Jesus had a demon and was mad, while others contended that he could not have a demon for he had healed the blind man.

58

Content

Precis (Mark 3:20-35)

The account begins with a crowd so large following Jesus and his disciples that they did not have time to eat. His family (or friends, according to some translations) tried to restrain him because they were afraid he was crazy. That was followed by an accusation that he was healing by the power of the prince of demons.

Jesus countered the scribes with the telling argument that the ruler of demons would not work against himself. Jesus then uses the example of invading a strong man's house. You could not do that unless you first bound him. Mark also includes the saying about the unforgivable sin as blaspheming the Holy Spirit.

The parable concludes with Jesus affirming that his real brothers and sisters are those who do the will of God. The implication is clear that he repudiates the attempts of his family to restrain him from doing what he believes is God's will for him.

Thesis: Jesus Christ as God's agent is stronger than the forces of evil in the world.

Theme: The followers of God in fellowship with Christ have the power to overcome evil.

Key Words in the Parable

1. "The Crowd." (v. 20) Many people were attracted by his healings and preaching. They followed him wherever he went, presumably at this point to Capernaum. It appears that he had moved his headquarters there from Nazareth.

2. "His family." (v. 21) The Greek is vague. It is not certain who is referred to here. Some translate it as "friends" (RSV). More accurate would be "those of his" which could be friends, family, his disciples or any associates.

3. "Gone Out of His Mind." (v. 21) This is a euphemism for being crazy. Were his friends or family concerned that he was in such a euphoric state over the reception he was receiving that he would exhaust himself? Or was it that his fanaticism was an embarrassment to them? The motives are not given. As usual, Mark only describes their actions.

4. "The Scribes ... from Jerusalem." (v. 22) This appears to be an official delegation of the doctors of the law. His actions caused them serious concern, since they had traveled all the way from Jerusalem to confront him.

5. "Beelzebul." (v. 22) The title is somewhat obscure. It probably refers to a deity in Syria and northern Palestine. It was considered to be a commander-in-chief of the demons. Some translate the term as the "lord of the mansion," which would lead to Jesus' comparison in the brief parable about entering the house of a strong man.

6. "Casts Out Demons." (v. 22) Jesus was considered to be an exorcist. Illness, especially mental illness, was believed to be caused by demon possession. An outside evil spirit had taken control of the person. Some superior force had to eject it for the person to be healed.

7. "How can Satan Cast out Satan?" (v. 23) Jesus identifies Beelzebul with Satan, the adversary of God. If Satan was trying to take possession of persons to establish his rule in the world, why would he allow one of his agents to overthrow his workers? Jesus reverses the argument and rebuts the scribes.

8. "A House." (vv. 25, 27) A house was used as an image for a political domain. In the Old Testament, for example, the continuation of the house of David represented the persistence of his dynasty as the rulers of Israel.

9. "His Property." (v. 27) What belongs to the devil? If creation is from God, nothing really belongs to the devil.

10. "Blaspheme." (vv. 28, 29) The term is not simply the use of bad language. That is to cheapen the word. It means to show lack of reverence or disrespect for God or to slander persons and ruin their reputation.

11. "Eternal Sin." (v. 29) The sin here is not so much a specific act but a state in which God is rejected and fellowship with him is broken permanently. To deny the work of the Holy Spirit is to refuse to be open to God's will in one's life.

12. "His Mother and His Brothers Came." (v. 31) His mother and brothers are identified in Mark 6:3 as Mary, James, Joses, Judas, and Simon. No sisters were mentioned by Mark as being with them in this instance. They had come down from Nazareth to Capernaum.

Contemplation

Issues and Insights

1. What is Strength? Many people confuse power, force and effort. Power is the ability to get something done. Force is the strength used to accomplish what one intends to do. Effort is the amount of energy expended to accomplish a task. Power and force need not be harmful, though the use of power or force is often assumed to be violent.

A basic power that people exercise is the consent they give to someone who is trying to get them to do something. People often consider themselves forced to do something when they give their consent to another's will. It is very hard for someone to "force" us to do anything when actually they can not do so unless we give some measure of consent to them.

Another person may pick us up and move us from one place to another, as when we "force" children not to play in the street by carrying them off the road. It is very difficult to make a person do something if he will not act in accord with our demands or wishes. The real problem most often is that we are not really "forced," but we don't want to accept the consequences of not doing what other persons want us to do. It then becomes an "imaginary constraint," not a real one.

In the same sense, Satan or the devil could not "force" Jesus to do his will. Jesus had already decided in the temptation experiences that he would only do God's will. That gave him the power to resist the enticements of the devil, even when it led to crucifixion. Out of his commitment to do God's will only came his unusual power.

2. The Unpardonable Sin. People from the Judaeo-Christian tradition often fear that they have committed the unpardonable sin. Persons with mental illness, especially those with depression, often have a sense of doom because they feel guilty of having committed the unpardonable sin. Actually, the fact that they have a sense of guilt and worry about the problem is a sign that they have not done so. The Holy Spirit is still active in them and they are responding.

The real unpardonable sin is when persons have become so calloused and have so frequently denied the promptings of conscience that they no longer feel any compunctions about sin. The news frequently comments about young people who hurt or kill people today and apparently have no regrets or remorse, no feelings of guilt. They may kill capriciously in drive-by shootings or as an act of initiation into a gang. It is these people whom we should be concerned about committing the unpardonable sin.

3. True Family. In this episode Jesus breaks clearly with Jewish tradition. They kept careful genealogical records to assure them that they were biologically connected to Abraham. Religion often was a matter of family relationships. To be part of the chosen people, a person had to have a genetic transmission of the convenantal promise.

Jesus challenged the biological basis of family when he turned from his mother and brothers who would try to dissuade him from doing God's will. Family is not a matter of biology primarily, but of kinship of faith, a spiritual relationship.

From this we can conclude that the church should be family. We have a spiritual kinship that binds us together. It should have priority over biological kinship. It is not a relationship that can easily relieve us of our obligation or connection to our family of origin. Indeed, Jesus on the cross was still sufficiently aware of his obligation to his mother that he commended her to the care of his disciples. His spiritual family became part of the obligation of his biological family. Does that tell us something about our mutual concern within the church?

4. Which God Do We Worship? Jesus was accused of worshipping Beelzebul. In practical terms, if he were doing the work of Beelzebul, then in actuality that was his god.

Our god is revealed by where we vest our highest values. What determines what we do shows our real loyalty, our real god. If we only do what our impulses and desires prompt us to do, we worship our own nature. If we pursue the values of money and property over persons, Mammon is the god we worship. If we see violence and the force of arms as the highest power, then Mars is our god. If the domination of people and political power is our highest value, than Satan is our god.

Jesus early in his ministry wrestled with the question of what he valued most. He was tempted repeatedly in his ministry to displace God's will with some other value as more important. Even his friends and his family urged him to restrain his unqualified dedication to doing God's will. He had to set his face steadfastly toward God and at times stand alone to show which God he really worshipped when tested.

If Jesus had to engage in this kind of struggle to worship the true God in practice, how much more do we need to test our own dedication to know which god we really worship?

5. Can Evil Cast Out Evil? Jesus' basic argument with the scribes was that evil cannot overcome evil. Only good can conquer evil. A fundamental issue that often faces people is to use evil means to do good.

We know in history that the war to end wars in World War I did not end wars. It laid the seeds that resulted in World War II.

Does violence get rid of violence? A basic axiom for many is that violence begets violence. A well-known cycle of retribution and revenge usually accompanies violence. Only when someone reverses the cycle by refusing to perpetuate the response of violence to violence and returns good for evil does the process end or become reversed.

Does killing someone to prove that killing is wrong really make the case? Or does it only afford evidence for persons to justify their own reasons for dealing with something that appears to them to be evil by removing it through killing the perpetrator or suspected perpetrator?

Many of the spiritual giants, such as Gandhi, Albert Schweitzer, Martin Luther King, Jr., and others were convinced that the moral structure of the universe is such that only good means can ultimately produce good results. You cannot defeat Satan by adopting Satan's means.

Homily Hints

1. Are You Crazy? (v. 21) To many people Christianity does not make sense. Those who take the teachings of Jesus seriously and try to live them must be somewhat odd or queer, if not out of their mind. The approach of science sometimes excludes such beliefs as the resurrection and the existence of personal beings other than people. They are considered absurdities.

    A. The Historical Experience — Explore the evidence of history for the effects of Christianity on those who believed and acted on apparent absurdities.

    B. The Limits of Science — Science as a method for gaining knowledge and understanding nature is eminently useful. When it goes beyond experiential and descriptive truth to more theoretical truth, science has limits.

    C. The Personal Experience — Faith has reasons which science cannot know.

2. The Pressure to Conformity. (vv. 21-22) Society wants to press us into a standard mold. The great advances of humanity have been made by those who dared to challenge the conventional wisdom. Jesus dared to challenge the scribes and Pharisees who wanted to pressure him to behave according to their standards. Where do Christians today need to live beyond the conventional wisdom?

 A. The Foolishness of Love — To love others is risky. It means you become vulnerable. But it has been the persons who have risked it who have changed people and accomplished great things in the world.

 B. The Paradoxes of Truth — What often seems contrary to conventional wisdom about human behavior has been life and society transforming.

 C. Models for a New World — The kingdom of God provides a different model for community than the world as we know it provides. To live it, people must be nonconformists.

3. The Temptation of the Ordinary. (vv. 31,32) It is easy to drift with the flow. To go against it requires a level of courage and commitment that may lead to difficulties.

 A. The Strength of Conviction

 B. The Power of Divine Conscience

 C. The Presence of Christ

4. Who is My Mother, Brother, Sister? (vv. 33-35)

 A. Kinship of Faith

 B. Identification with the Needy

 C. The Church as True Family

5. The Sin Against the Holy Spirit. (vv. 28-30)

 A. Sensitivity to the Spirit — Seeking to be open to the prompting of the Holy Spirit is assurance that we have not sinned against it.

 B. Acting on Truth — As we seriously act on the truth as we perceive it, more and more certain truth is revealed to us.

C. Strength Added Daily — We do not gain strength and courage in one fell swoop usually. It comes as we exercise what we already have.

Contact

Points of Contact

1. Experiencing Family. Everyone longs for human companionship. People want to be accepted and appreciated. It is difficult to stand out from the crowd and be different. Someone has said that personal failures are always failures of love. The church should be a true family where people find acceptance and experience love. The church should be a family where people's differences are not cause for rejection but for understanding. The church should be a place for support, especially for those who are struggling to deal with their sin and seeking to know and courage to do the will of God.

The church as family needs to allow persons to have honest doubt as they search for truth and in the search to test different ways in seeking to know the will of God for them. The church needs to be careful in placing restraints on people who are seriously seeking the truth and the will of God. It needs to be cautious that it does not act as did the friends and family of Jesus because they do not understand the person who has a different calling to do the will of God.

2. A Surrogate Family. In the American culture the family experiences much strain and stress. One marriage in two currently ends in divorce. Mobility and anonymity of the urban and industrial societies often remove many of the supporting structures of a stable community.

Typical ways of dealing with conflict that develop in stable communities disappear when community is absent. The recourse to the legal system tends to alienate and antagonize persons in conflicts. The adversarial nature of the American judicial process drives people apart rather than reconciling them.

The church should develop skills and provide services for the family. It should work as a surrogate family to counsel and mediate so that people are held together; where the conflict leads to breakdown, to try to make the separations as amicable as possible rather than being filled with hostility and bitterness.

3. Devil Worship and Demon Possession. Movies such as *The Exorcist* and reports of devil worship probably have people unsettled. False images of the devil, fostered by such representations as occur at Halloween, lead people to dismiss too easily the reality of the forces of evil.

Forces are at work which tend to lead people to evil. People become obsessed with certain ideas that are demonic. Some people become so enmeshed in fear and hate that they cannot extricate themselves from them. They are compelled to strike out against what they fear and hate. They make objects of their fear and hate into demons. They can then justify destroying them with any and every means imaginable.

Others feel the forces of evil are so strong that they cannot deny them. So, following the adage that if you can't beat them, join them, they worship these powers.

The church offers an alternative. It sees the forces of good, it offers hope of conquest over the powers of evil, it has the resources to overcome hatred and fear. It needs both to offer these resources and to demonstrate their reality in overcoming the structure and forces of evil that are real. To do so, it must recognize the reality of the evil and not trivialize it with a false image of the devil as a creature with horns and a forked tail and dressed in red flannel underwear!

4. Eternal Life and Death. Eternal life or death is not time extended indefinitely, and only after the death of the body. They are states of existence, qualities of life that are not factors of time. They are not something to wait for in a later heaven or hell. They are where we now are living and point to our continued existence.

Those who deny the true meaning of their humanity, who are sinking to the level of the demonic, are already living in hell and are experiencing eternal death. Those who know the reality of the living Christ and the action of the Holy Spirit in disclosing to them the will of God and aiding them in living now in the kingdom of God are already enjoying eternal life.

The direction of the movement of our life, either to death or to life of the spirit, shows us where we will end. We already have apprehensions of our part in the totality of existence, whether we are part of the good or the evil. How we act in the flesh has a determinative effect on what we are becoming, whether to eternal life or eternal death.

Illustrative Materials

1. Exorcism. The news recently carried the story of parents who battered their son to death to try to cast out demons from him. They succumbed to their fears about what they had brought to life and lacked assurance that they could cope with the responsibility to raise him to the life of goodness.

2. The Dual Nature of Persons. A student once wrote on an exam that man has a *duel* nature. People do have within them the capacity for good and evil. They are, in effect, a house which can be inhabited by two strong men who duel with each other. They need to open themselves to the forces that will bind the strong man of evil impulses and give victory to the strong presence of Christ.

3. Brothers and Sisters in Christ. A group of churches in south Germany only uses the title of brother and sister for members of their churches. They do not use the German equivalents of Mr., Mrs., or Reverend for each other. The children who are not yet of age to be members of the church call church members who are not their parents uncles and aunts. The church is regarded as an extended family.

4. Who are True Parents?
A. A minister and his wife had two biological children and an adopted child. The minister contended that true parents are not

necessarily those who give birth to a child. He proposed that many women who never gave birth to a child nevertheless were truer mothers to many children than the birth mothers. They usually were teachers who loved and helped children to realize their fullest possibilities. People who give love and help others come to flower may be truer parents than the parents of origin who abuse and neglect their children.

B. The news has had several stories in recent years where the law has tried to decide who had the right to custody of a child. A few cases involved children who were given up at birth for adoption. In at least two cases the biological father, who was not married to the mother, tried much later to reverse the decision of the mother to give the child up for adoption. In one instance two babies were exchanged at birth and the mistake was discovered after the death of one of the two children. Who are the true parents in such cases?

C. Custody battles in divorce often do not show that either parent really has the child's welfare at heart. The child becomes a pawn in the antagonisms of the parents. The issue is not what is best for the child but who wins the battle between the parents. What is the true parent?

5. Casting Out Demons. The novel by George Orwell, *1984,* proposed that the future society would have as slogans: IGNORANCE IS STRENGTH, SLAVERY IS FREEDOM and WAR IS PEACE. Twisting of falsehood, slavery and war into goods are samples of Satan casting out demons. But can demons be used to cast out demons?

5. Seeds And The Kingdom

Mark 4:26-34

---

²⁶*He also said, "The kingdom of God is as if someone would scatter seed on the ground, ²⁷and would sleep and rise night and day, and the seed would sprout and grow, he does not know how. ²⁸The earth produces of itself, first the stalk, then the head, then the full grain in the head. ²⁹But when the grain is ripe, at once he goes in with his sickle, because the harvest has come."*

³⁰*He also said, "With what can we compare the kingdom of God, or what parable will we use for it? ³¹It is like a mustard seed, which, when sown upon the ground, is the smallest of all the seeds on earth; ³²yet when it is sown it grows up and becomes the greatest of all shrubs, and puts forth large branches, so that the birds of the air can make nests in its shade."*

³³*With many such parables he spoke the word to them, as they were able to hear it; 34he did not speak to them except in parables, but he explained everything in private to his disciples.*

At this writing the U.S. House of Representatives has just completed its 100 days of legislation on the so-called Contract with America. It was an effort to change quickly a process which was at work through several decades. Some analysts criticize the legislation for having been put together too hastily. It was driven by a desire to demonstrate instant results.

The probability is that the legislation will move through the Senate with more "deliberate speed." The Senate will look more closely to discern whether the legislation will bring with it unintended results. The effects of the proposals may not have been sufficiently considered.

The disciples may well have expected that the preaching and activity of Jesus would produce immediate results in the coming of the kingdom. They may have been impatient for him to bring the kingdom instantaneously. Indeed, among the temptations of Jesus was to try to force the coming of the kingdom by some magical act of power. He made a deliberate choice to go the slower way that is analogous to the planting of seed, allowing it to germinate and eventually grow into the fruit of the harvest.

Jesus frequently drew on the images of farming to illustrate his understanding of how the kingdom develops in history. He had the patience to take the time to let his processes work their way to fruition. He could do so because he was confident that they were in accord with the reality of God's working through life to certain results despite the apparent contradictions when seen in a short-range view.

Context

Context of the Season

We are at the fourth Sunday after Pentecost. It is in the midst of the growing season for much of North America. It is a time of waiting for crops to mature. The seeds were planted earlier. In the Corn Belt the typical farmer would expect the corn to be "knee high by the Fourth of July."

For the church, much of the activity is engaged in the process of cultivating the Christian life. It is the long, steady time between the high events of the church year. What the pastor needs to do is to sustain the development of people's spirituality as they grow in fuller understanding of the life and teachings of Jesus, and as they apply them to their life and the world in which they live.

Context of the Lectionary

The First Lesson. (1 Samuel 15:34—16:13) Samuel had concluded that Saul was no longer qualified to be king. A successor who was more in accord with God's desire for a king over Israel was needed. Fearful of Saul's reaction if he knew what Samuel was doing, Samuel went searching on the pretext of offering a sacrifice. The choice of Saul as king was made at least in part because he was a striking figure and stood head and shoulders above the crowd. Samuel felt that the next choice should be someone with the inner strength of character to be king rather than the size (see 1 Samuel 16:7). After examining each of Jesse's sons, he came to the one whom Jesse thought would be the least likely choice. Saul anointed David as his choice to be the next king.

The Second Lesson. (2 Corinthians 5:6-10, 14-17) Paul would prefer to be free from the limitations of the flesh and to be fully at home with his Lord. Nevertheless he had continuing work to do so he looks at his course from Christ's point of view rather than from the human perspective. Just as Samuel looked at the choice of a king from God's way of evaluating him, Paul looks at the world from the whole new creation which God is seeking to bring into being.

Gospel. (Mark 4:26-34) Jesus tells two parables to help the disciples understand the nature of the coming of the kingdom. It does not enter into history by some divine and spectacular intervention. It comes more like the growth of life from a seed to full maturity. Despite the slow process the results are both large and sure.

Psalm. (Psalm 20) The psalm is one of prayer for help for the king. It ends with assurance that God will support the leader. The psalm connects with the lessons which deal with issues of leadership. It connects with the Gospel reading in the expectation of the two parables that the results of God's kingdom will be great.

Context of the Scripture

The parable of the growth of the seed is one of two which are only found in Mark. Matthew and Luke have other parables that are somewhat similar but not identical.

Mark uses the word "parable" twelve times in his gospel (3:23; 4:2, 10, 11, 13, 33, 34; 7:17; 12:1, 12, 13; 13:28). Ten of the twelve are found in Matthew and Luke. In addition to the one today, another found only in Mark is 13:34-37.

Context of Related Scriptures

> Ezekiel 17:23-24 — A twig of cedar planted by God will grow so that every kind of bird will live in its branches.
> Daniel 4:10-12 — A vision of a tree so tall its top reached to heaven and birds nested in its branches.
> Joel 3:13 — The call to put in the ripened harvest.
> Matthew 13:24-30 — The parable of the weeds.
> Matthew 13:31-33; Luke 13:18-19 — The parable of the mustard seed.
> Matthew 17:20; Luke 17:5 — Faith the size of a mustard seed.
> John 4:35-38 — The fields are ripe for harvest.
> 1 Corinthians 3:6-7 — Various persons plant or water, but God gives the growth.
> James 5:7-8 — Be patient as a farmer who waits for the precious crop.
> Revelation 14:14-20 — The angels using the sickle for harvest.

Content

Precis (Mark 4:26-34)

A parable is told to illustrate the nature of the kingdom of God. A farmer sows the seed. Then he waits to allow it to germinate, sprout, grow to maturity when it puts forth the heads for grain, and then the head ripens. Only at that point does the farmer again become active by cutting the plants to reap the harvest.

A second parable about the nature of the kingdom of God also comes from agriculture. The kingdom of God begins so small that it is like the smallest of seeds. The seed has within it the coding that results in the growth of a plant large enough so that birds can build nests in it.

74

Jesus spoke his many parables publicly to large crowds. It was his normal way of addressing them. He explains them fully to his disciples in private. He does this to prepare them for a larger role in leadership later.

Thesis: The coming of the kingdom has the same mysterious but persistent growth characteristic of life.

Theme: Exercise patience and hope in waiting for kingdom results.

Key Words in the Parable

1. "Someone." (v. 26) It is not clear from the parable to whom Jesus referred as the farmer. Is the sower God, Jesus or anyone who proclaims the coming of the kingdom of God? Probably it implies that the sower is any Christian who by word or deed testifies to the presence of the kingdom of God.

2. "Scatter Seed." (v. 26) The seed is the word of God which is made manifest to people. It has to be spread abroad so that others may receive and respond to it.

3. "Sleep and Rise." (v. 27) The point is the length of time for planting to bring results. Kingdom growth is not to be forced. It requires patient waiting for the results to appear.

4. "Sprout and Grow." (v. 27) A seed, once planted, does not immediately produce harvest. The farmer can observe its progress but it takes time before the results come.

5. "The Earth Produces of Itself." (v. 28) The Greek word for "produces of itself" is the same word transliterated in English as "automatic." We do not make seeds grow and produce the harvest. So, too, we scatter the seed. The Holy Spirit is at work producing the results as naturally as seeds sprouting and growing when the conditions are right.

6. "When the Grain is Ripe." (v. 29) Here it is implied that time is not simply chronological. Certain moments are of more significance than others. Results come at the right time.

7. "He Goes in with His Sickle." (v. 29) It is unclear from the parable who reaps the harvest. In other passages in the Gospels, it appears that Christians are to help bring in the harvest. Elsewhere it appears that the harvest is eschatalogical — at the end of time.

8. "A Mustard Seed." (v. 31) The emphasis is on a seed that is small but with large potential. The point is not the value of the seed or the fruitfulness of it, but the contrast of its size with the size of the plant it produces. The mustard seed is not the one from which we get Grey Poupon!

9. "The Smallest of All Seeds." (v. 31) The seed is not actually the smallest of all seeds but was proverbially considered to be so. Any gardener knows that some seeds are so fine that you can hardly scatter them far enough apart to allow proper space to grow. The gardener will mix them with sand so as to "dilute" them.

10. "Birds ... Make Nests in its Shade." (v. 32) Be careful about allegorizing the parable. Some early interpretations saw the branches of the shrub as denominations and the birds as false sects that arose in Christian communities. It is almost certain that the only point Jesus intended was the exaggerated size of the outcome from small and not very pretentious beginnings.

11. "Able to Hear It." (v. 33) Jesus fashioned his message according to the condition of his hearers. He was an expert in mass communication, casting his message in a form that everyone could grasp and remember even if they did not fully comprehend its meaning at the moment.

Contemplation

Issues and Insights

1. The Kingdom and History. Two different views of the nature of the coming of the kingdom in history have developed from this parable. Some would press the image of "first the stalk, then the head, then the full grain in the head" (v. 28) to refer to various dispensations. History moves from the dispensation of Law to the dispensation of Gospel to the dispensation of the Spirit. Law would be the Old Testament or Israel; Gospel would be the New Testament or the church; and the Spirit is the age yet to come and usher in the end of history.

Others would place the emphasis on the automatic nature of the kingdom of God. They see history as evolutionary. Religion moves through a series of stages as mankind understands better what it is about. It started with animism, progressed to polytheism, and on to henotheism until it reached monotheism. We are arriving at the highest stage of understanding with ethical monotheism.

The question is whether both of these are reading more into the parable than Jesus ever intended that should be gotten out of it. If we accept the fundamental principle that a parable is usually to make a single point, should we rather accept that the major teaching was that the kingdom is not coming in spectacular and magical ways? Is it not more of a gradual growth as people come to accept it as the true nature and meaning of human life?

2. The Results Will Come. When one reads the newspapers or watches television, the amount of evil in the world seems to be overwhelming. The news reports catalogue the ills afflicting humankind. They are filled with war, crime, natural disasters, violence, poverty, bankruptcy, sickness and death. It is sometimes hard to find any evidence of the kingdom of God in our midst.

Jesus certainly could look about him in Palestine and see evidence that the kingdom was not very fully realized. Despite his growing popularity, the task of trying to change the circumstances

77

of people seemed overwhelming. Progress toward the establishment of the kingdom seemed very slow. His followers might well have become discouraged.

The parables give both perspective and hope about the nature of the coming of the kingdom. On the one hand, they call for patience while waiting for results to come. A farmer can sow the seed and try to set the conditions to encourage growth. Still, he can only wait for the forces to work automatically according to the nature of the seed and to bring forth life in its own time.

On the other hand, life is persistent. Despite all the obstacles to the fulfillment of life, it is persistent. The results are abundant. Since the very nature of its being accords with what is real and true, the kingdom of God must persist and its results will come.

Therefore the disciples and Christians work with confidence that the kingdom of God is coming. We need not be discouraged in the face of slow progress. The parable calls for continuing to scatter the seed, confident that God will produce the harvest in abundance.

3. Surprises in History. Humble and unlikely beginnings often have amazing results.

Who could have guessed in advance that the actions of a merchant's son who took the vow of poverty and went about the country as a beggar would lead to a movement of spirituality that saved the church for the city in the thirteenth century? St. Francis of Assisi generated a popular movement which still inspires many people.

Who would have guessed that the posting of 95 issues for academic debate about the nature of indulgences would spark a movement known as the Protestant Reformation? It is almost certain that Luther did not anticipate the implications of what he was doing. He probably did not want to break with the medieval church but rather correct it. He certainly could not have conceived of the extent of the consequences of that act.

Did Rosa Parks have any idea of the changes that would be wrought because she refused to move to the back of the bus in Montgomery, Alabama? The unleashing of the civil rights movement that reached even beyond the issue of race to the place of women in modern society and many other civil rights concerns were not in her mind when she insisted on the simple right of justice.

It was hard to imagine ten years ago that a prisoner serving a life term on Robben Island would lead South Africa to a multiracial government. All the predictions in the early 1980s anticipated a lengthy and bloody process with an uncertain outcome for that country.

In all these cases the seed fell into fertile soil. The conditions were right for the growth of the kingdom. Where will the seed be planted today in some simple act of faithfulness that will produce large and surprising results by the coming of the kingdom into history?

4. Salvation Includes Growth. Salvation comes both in an immediate sense but also by growth. At some point in life a person must respond directly to God's grace and be formed anew or regenerated by the power of the Holy Spirit. At that point life receives a new direction. Instead of being propelled toward death by pride and self-interest, the person now moves in the direction of life and sanctification.

After the seed of the word has been planted and has sprouted, it must continue to grow to produce the stalk, the head and the full grain in the head. That should be an ongoing process of maturation in the Christian life.

In like manner a young church will probably first put its emphasis on calling people to the new life in Christ. As it grows it should move on to add to that thrust the growth in community that shows in its life all the teaching of Jesus, reaching out to manifest the coming of the kingdom of God in all its personal and social relationships.

The church, both in the life of its members and its corporate life, should produce the fruits of proclaiming the gospel, teaching the full implications of it, and healing the ills of evil and injustices around and within it.

1. The Patient Farmer. (vv. 26-29)
A. Faithfully Sowing the Seed
B. Cultivating Conditions for Growth
C. Waiting for God to Give the Increase
D. Bringing in the Harvest

2. The Harvest Will Come. (v. 29)
What is the activity of the church in putting in the sickle to bring in the harvest? When does it come?
A. Watching for Growth. After proclaiming the Gospel the need is to wait for signs of response.
B. Timing of the Invitation. Persons who are ready to respond need to be invited but not unduly pressured to come into fellowship of the church.
C. Leaving the Final Harvest to God. Judgment about who is ultimately saved is God's prerogative, not ours.

3. The End is in the Beginning. (vv. 31-32)
A. The Beginning Point May be Small. The spoken word may seem insignificant but can be powerful.
B. The Outcome Depends on the Beginning. Only good means serve to bring good results despite apparent consequences otherwise.
C. Hope for the Harvest. Faith includes the trust that God will produce the harvest even when we cannot see far enough to see all the outcomes.

4. Speaking the Word. (vv. 26, 33-34)
A. The Seed Must be Scattered. The word needs to be proclaimed. People need to be confronted with God's claims and promises of grace.
B. Speaking to the People. The level of the message needs to be where the people are.
C. Explaining Everything. As people are ready to receive and understand, Christians should move beyond the simple gospel to the understanding of all things Jesus taught.

5. Expect Great Results. (vv. 31-32)
A. Do we Expect Too Little?
B. Dare to Venture for Large Results.
C. Place Your Trust in God's Outcome.

Contact

Points of Contact

1. An Antidote to Discouragement. Christians may become depressed and discouraged when they pray that God's kingdom will come on earth. If they do not see results of their efforts to live the Christian life and to build the church, they may despair that the gospel is not effective.

The two parables were given to encourage the people of Jesus' time when prospects that the kingdom was coming probably seemed bleak. Again and again in history the coming of the kingdom seems to be losing ground. Governments have exerted great pressures to root out Christianity all the way from the Roman emperors to the Communist regimes of modern times.

Even when the institutional church has become corrupted and it has appeared that the church was going to collapse from within, new movements have generated new life. A recovered vitality has renewed the life of Christians and given the church new influence in the world.

The parables suggest both patience in times of discouragement and hope for great results to come. People need to have the messages of both the parables as an antidote to discouragement and despair.

2. Expectations of Maturity. A frequent question in the church concerns the role of nurture in Christian faith. When should we expect people to be ready to respond to Christ's invitation? How much pressure should you exert on persons to assume the full responsibilities of Christian living?

Children need to be nourished and supported. They need to be prepared for the time when the faith becomes their own. The seed has to be planted and as it sprouts in the life of persons, they need to be supported. At some point the fruit needs to be harvested. Sometimes it becomes almost automatic at a certain age as a rite of passage. Not everyone matures at the same rate, however, or responds in the same way. People need to be confronted with choice, but a danger is that if they feel forced they may go through the motions but the experience may not be real. They then may be "inoculated" against the real thing.

Some people may find certain moments or experiences critical for moving from one stage to another. It may be some experience of illumination when the Holy Spirit makes clear to them another stage for their spiritual development. For some it may be a significant decision which they confront. It may be a career choice, the question of marriage, the birth of a child with its attendant responsibilities. It may be in facing some ethical choice or some personal behavior that needs to be changed.

We should encourage people to consider and celebrate as they grow to maturity. A decisive moment which begins the Christian life is not the final goal. We should expect that growth will be a lifelong process and encourage persons to confront from time to time how they move to greater maturing in Christian living.

3. Looking for the Harvest. God is active in history bringing forth new fruit. Church members can be challenged to look at where new growth is appearing or is needed. If they can exercise faith they can help to move the growth ahead.

Occasionally we become aware of some blind spot that persons or society have. We need to be sensitive to the developments that make the times ready to attack such problems. Church members should look about and try to identify where people are hurting and no one is doing anything about it. They should ask what the equivalents are today for giving sight to the blind, making the lame to walk, releasing the prisoner, feeding the hungry and clothing the naked.

The church has most frequently tackled both personal and social problems. It has noted the hurts and moved to heal and help. The Holy Spirit has helped Christians to realize their full personhood as they have reached out to meet the needs of others. The world needs the harvest of righteousness which changes the conditions that prevent persons from achieving their full possibilities.

4. Postponed Harvest. We live in an age of expectations of instant solutions. We have instant soups, instant coffee and tea, instant TV dinners, and instant solutions to complex problems or situations on television. This mood tends to lead people to want instant gratification.

When society was largely agrarian, people knew that it took time from the planting of seed until the harvest arrived. Results from efforts and activities came slowly. People had to wait for postponed consequences.

Jesus admonished the multitudes and his disciples to act in faithfulness to the will of God even though the results seem to be delayed in coming. The kingdom of God is often hidden in its results. People need to learn to be patient in their hope but trusting that God is in control and active. The harvest is sure and will be plentiful in God's good time.

Illustrative Materials

1. Surprising Harvest. In our garden some tomato plants appeared in the compost heap. We were unaware of having had cherry tomatoes. Nevertheless two or three plants grew, prospered, and produced a substantial crop which we enjoyed. On another occasion a peculiar looking growth appeared on some vines in the midst of our zucchini. To our surprise some very tasty cantaloupes eventually matured on those vines. They apparently grew from seeds in garbage we had buried the previous summer to use as fertilizer. God sometimes causes sprouts to arise and produce fruits where we are unaware of planting seeds!

2. The Miracle of Growth.
A. It is a miracle that in a seed so small as to be invisible to the naked eye encoded DNA carries a message that will produce a human being. The amazing talents of a Mozart, an Einstein, a

Madame Curie, or a Florence Nightingale are potential in this small package. All the diversity and riches of human life with its great potential come from such small but very complicated beginnings.

B. The baby panda at birth weighs only about 2.5-5 ounces. It grows to be as much as a 220 pound adult. That is at birth one nine-hundreth of the weight of an adult panda. An elephant can grow from a baby of 200 pounds at birth to a mature animal of up to six tons. A whale weighs about 2.5 tons at birth. An adult blue whale weighs as much as 160 tons and can be 100 feet in length.

3. The Persistence of Life. Despite all that can threaten and destroy it, life is very persistent. We probably do not often think of bacteria as a form of life. Yet it is a life form that constantly struggles to stay alive.

We recently have become aware that tuberculosis has developed resistance to all the antibiotics that scientists have devised. As the bacteria have become resistant to one form of antibiotic, scientists found another to be effective. Each time the bacteria has adapted and some of them escaped to come back resistant and more virulent than before. While we do not like these forms of life, they do illustrate the persistence of life.

In a somewhat similar and surprising way, two children were born of mothers who had the HIV infection. The babies gave evidence of having the infection at birth. Doctors expected that these children would eventually contract AIDS and probably have a short life. Instead, at five years of age these children show no trace of HIV infection. Life shows ability to resist the threat to it.

4. Forcing the Kingdom. People from time to time try to bring the Kingdom of God by force. In the sixteenth century certain self-proclaimed prophets expected God to install his kingdom in the city of Strasbourg. The prophet was imprisoned and the kingdom did not seem to be coming there. Then some of the followers found the city of Münster receptive to their preaching. They concluded that they were mistaken both in the place and the way the kingdom was to come. They decided Münster was the place and that they should take over the city. They forced those who did not agree to leave the city. When it was attacked by opposing forces they defended it with weapons as they prepared to receive the kingdom. Instead, they were defeated and the attempt ended in disaster. Their fall smeared other peaceful efforts to live the pure Christian life and led any who did so to be suspected of going the way of the Münsterites.

The Crusades trying to liberate the Holy Land as God's will for the Christian church resulted in equally disastrous results. The crusaders ended up fighting more among themselves than against the Moslems. Even today much of the so-called "Christian West" activity in intervening in the Middle East and north Africa is branded as a new crusade. Moslems view such activity as another Christian effort to bring the kingdom by force instead of by the slower but more certain way of planting the seed, watching the growth patiently, and waiting for God to bring the harvest.

6. Bread For Life

John 6:35, 41-51

---

³⁵Jesus said to them, "I am the bread of life. Whoever comes to me will never be hungry, and whoever believes in me will never be thirsty."
⁴¹Then the Jews began to complain about him because he said, "I am the bread that came down from heaven."
⁴²They were saying, "Is not this Jesus, the son of Joseph, whose father and mother we know? How can he now say, 'I have come down from heaven'?" ⁴³Jesus answered them, "Do not complain among yourselves. ⁴⁴No one can come to me unless drawn by the Father who sent me; and I will raise that person up on the last day. ⁴⁵It is written in the prophets, 'And they shall all be taught by God.' Everyone who has heard and learned from the Father comes to me. ⁴⁶Not that anyone has seen the Father except the one who is from God; he has seen the Father. ⁴⁷Very truly, I tell you, whoever believes has eternal life. ⁴⁸I am the bread of life. ⁴⁹Your ancestors ate the manna in the wilderness, and they died. ⁵⁰This is the bread that comes down from heaven, so that one may eat of it and not die. ⁵¹I am the living bread that came down from heaven. Whoever eats of this bread will live forever; and the bread that I will give for the life of the world is my flesh."

Friends told me recently that they had bought a bread-making machine. Such machines cost from under $100 on up. They can bake a wide variety of breads depending on the type of machine bought. They can make one to two pound loaves in a couple hours, or you can set the more expensive ones to bake over a longer period of time and have fresh baked bread ready when you want it.

Some people would not think of using a bread-making machine where you only put in the ingredients and the machine does the rest. They like to knead the dough and shape the loaves themselves. They get pleasure out of the bread-making process.

Jesus uses the familiarity and importance of bread that supports life to make a point about his own mission. In John 6 Jesus uses the word "bread" seventeen times according to the NRSV translation and in addition has four references to "loaves." He came to people to feed them. He did not hesitate to provide bread for the physical body when that seemed necessary. He even defended the right of his disciples to pick grain from the field on the Sabbath and to eat it raw when they were hungry and had no food available.

More important was Jesus' mission to feed the soul. He knew the hunger of people to know their true destiny. They needed to know the full meaning of their life. He offered them an understanding of the full significance of humanity and the way to experience it. In that larger sense he made the claim to be the bread of life (John 6:35) or the living bread (John 6:51).

Context

Context of the Gospel according to John

The account of the feeding of the 5,000 appears in all of the synoptic gospels. It is one of the few accounts other than the last week of Jesus' life which the Gospel according to John shares with them, assuming that the feeding of the crowd here is the same event. The feeding increased the expectations of the people. After the feeding they followed him around the Sea of Galilee.

Jesus tried in an extended discourse to use the interest aroused by the feeding to move the people beyond their awareness of physical food to the need for spiritual feeding. John places the chapter as a centerpiece of Jesus' ministry to the masses.

Context of the Lectionary

As is customary, this is the third Sunday in sequence with a part of John 6 as the Gospel reading. This section and next Sunday's, which conclude the series, are two of the parables or extended metaphors in the chapter. It is appropriate to devote this attention to John 6 since, as noted, this is the longest discourse by Jesus before the last week according to John's account. It also is a turning point in the Gospel account. The chapter ends by saying that the disciples found Jesus' statement difficult and some turned back from following him.

The First Lesson. (2 Samuel 18:5-9, 15, 31-33) The reading reports the death of Absalom despite David's entreaty that he be dealt with gently. The Cushite who brought David the report of Absalom's death assumed that David would be pleased since it ended a rebellion against him. Instead David grieves at the death of his son.

The Second Lesson. (Ephesians 4:25—5:2) Paul advises the Ephesians on how they should live the new life in Christ. Much of what is contained in these instructions are elaborations of Jesus' teaching in the Sermon on the Mount.

Gospel. (John 6:35, 41-51) Jesus uses the symbolism of bread to call his followers to partake of his example and teachings to nourish their spiritual life. Whereas physical bread feeds the flesh that is corruptible, his bread feeds the spirit which endures eternally.

Psalm. (Psalm 130) The psalm begins with a plea for redemption. It proceeds through the affirmation that the psalmist waits with longing for redemption to the expression of hope that the power and love of God will lead to the redemption of Israel.

Context of Related Scriptures

> Genesis 3:19 — The judgment that people would eat bread by the sweat of their face.
> Exodus 16:13-33 — The account of manna provided in the wilderness.

Numbers 11:4-9 — The people grumble because they only have manna to eat and not the familiar foods from Egypt.

1 Kings 17:8-16 — Elijah fed bread by the widow of Zarephath.

Psalm 78:23-25 — God commands the heaven for all to open and rain manna, the bread of angels, on the Israelites.

Mark 6:31-44; Matthew 14:13-21; Luke 9:10-17 — Parallel passages which tell of the feeding of the 5,000.

Mark 8:1-10; Matthew 15:32-39 — The feeding of the 4,000.

1 Corinthians 10:1-4 — Paul alludes to the spiritual food and drink which the Israelites imbibed in the wilderness.

Content

Precis (John 6:35, 41-51)

Jesus makes the first of his "I am" claims by asserting that he is the bread of life. As he had earlier offered the Samaritan woman at the well living water that would never lead her to thirst again (John 4:13-14), he now offers bread that will not leave a person hungry or thirsty ever again. When the Jews complain about his claim that he has come down from heaven, Jesus reiterates his claim and indeed heightens it by saying that his bread is superior to the manna in the wilderness. His living bread can nourish for eternal life.

Thesis: Partaking of Jesus as the living bread leads to eternal life.

Theme: Identity with the person of Jesus is real life.

Key Words in the Parable

1. "Bread of Life." (v. 35) Jesus uses a staple food that sustains life to call people to respond to his teachings which will nourish the life of the spirit.

2. "Never be Hungry ... Thirsty." (v. 35) These phrases clearly echo Isaiah's promise of God to Israel in Isaiah 49:8-10.

3. "Came Down from Heaven." (vv. 41, 51) John repeats the theme announced in John 1:1-18. Jesus as the Word (*Logos*) is of divine origin.

4. "Son of Joseph." (v. 42) The Jews have no awareness of a claim of virgin birth here. They assume that they know the earthly parentage of Jesus so his claim seems to them absurd.

5. "Drawn by the Father." (v. 44) Salvation is not initially the activity of persons. They come to salvation because of the initial attraction of them by God.

6. "It is Written in the Prophets." (v. 45) No doubt a reference to Jeremiah 31:33. Jesus was steeped in the scriptures of the Old Testament so that he quoted them frequently.

7. "Taught by God." (v. 45) Jeremiah called for a new covenant written on the heart. Jesus contrasts the law which was given to Moses, written on stone and taught by the rabbis, with the spiritual understanding of those who receive it directly from God.

8. "Seen the Father ... Except the One from God." (v. 46) Again John repeats a theme from the prologue to his gospel account. John 1:18 says "No one has ever seen God. It is God the only Son ... who has made him known." This is at least an indirect claim of the identity of Jesus with the Son and therefore also identical with God.

9. "Whoever Believes has Eternal Life." (v. 47) Here again is a central theme in John's account. Eternal life is not something given after death but is already experienced in life in the world. It is not so much a measure of the length of life as it is a state of being, a quality of living.

10. "I am the Bread of Life." (v. 48) This affirmation is a repetition of v. 35. It is one of the numerous symbolic uses of language in John's account to establish the nature of Jesus.

11. "Ate the Manna in the Wilderness, and they Died." (v. 49) Again John contrasts the physical with the spiritual and uses Old Testament figures as a basis for comparison and contrast with Jesus. By implication Jesus is a different and superior type from Moses.

12. "The Bread I will Give for the Life of the World is My Flesh." (v. 51) Once again John plays on a theme from the prologue where it is announced that the Word became flesh (John 1:14). Here is both the theme of Jesus' incarnation and self-sacrifice for the world.

Contemplation

Issues and Insights

1. The Passover Connection. In John 6:4, John notes that the feeding of the crowd and discourses on bread occurred as the Passover was near. The question arises as to whether he sees Jesus as a new deliverer who becomes the sacrifice for the people and who offers a bread better than the manna in the wilderness. The Jews believed that the new Messiah would bring a renewing of the manna.

Can we reinterpret the Passover legitimately as an event that must occur in every life? Is it no longer just an experience of the deliverance of the Hebrew people from slavery as an historical event? But must it be a personal experience of each person? Each person must go through a wilderness experience that leads to a belief and trust in the living bread that is far better than the manna in the wilderness.

2. The Physical and the Spiritual. Jesus rebukes the crowd for coming to him primarily because they had received physical food when they were hungry. The real hunger of people is spiritual. The physical food gives immediate pleasure and temporary sustenance. To find the real meaning of life by responding to the action of God provides an enduring and real sustenance for living.

Though not directly included in the passage for today, the earlier section suggests that the feeding of the crowd led to a renewed temptation experience for Jesus. John does not record the temptations as given in the synoptic gospels. In John 6 Jesus is tempted to become a king (v. 15) and to continue to provide food miraculously (vv. 26, 30). Jesus turns the desires of the crowd from physical hunger and thirst to the need to receive spiritual food by coming to him and believing in him (v. 35). Because Jesus had at the beginning of his public ministry faced and rejected temptations to engage in the wrong kinds of ministry, he could now understand the desires of the crowd. He tries to redirect their desires away from the wrong means to the right spiritual means.

3. The Incarnation in Reverse. In Jesus the Word became flesh and dwelt among the people of Palestine. From the Latin word for flesh *(carnes)* comes the word for the doctrine of incarnation. Jesus manifested the degree to which the divine could be clothed in flesh and revealed most fully what the divine means in human beings.

Jesus calls those who come to him to accept him and his teachings and thus, in a sense, to enter into a reversal of the incarnation. As the Word became flesh as it came down from heaven and took on human form, people are to allow the word of God to enter their flesh by believing in the person and teachings of Jesus. In that way, to the degree that people manifest the same life as found in Jesus, the incarnation is reversed. Those who have been dominated by the desires of the flesh are enabled to be fed by the Spirit and show the divine in their life.

4. Divine Instruction as Bread. In Jewish thinking the Old Testament story of manna coming down from heaven was symbolic of divine instruction. It is God's teaching that nourishes the soul in a way similar to bread feeding the body. An issue which some raise is whether Jesus is saying that his teachings are divine instruction.

93

A question then arises as to whether Jesus meant that the bread he offers was his teaching that came down from heaven. Or is it the person of Jesus who came down from heaven? If the Word became flesh, can the flesh become the divine word as people take Christ and his teachings into their life? Can they become revealers of the divine teachings to others?

Contemplation

Bread is a source of energy and growth. Runners who want to store up energy for a race eat a high carbohydrate diet. Bread is one of the major sources for such energy. Bread also sustains growth.

Persons who want to grow spiritually need to partake of the life, example, and teachings of Jesus. He shares with those who enter into fellowship with him and believe in him an abundance of rich spiritual gifts.

Bread is eaten daily by much of the world's population. It provides strength for the day's work. In like manner persons need regularly, preferably daily, to meditate and think about the teachings of Jesus and his presence in their lives. Thus they too can be strengthened spiritually for their work and can grow into his likeness.

Homily Hints

1. An End to Hunger. (v. 35)
A. Hunger and Thirst after Righteousness
B. Feed on the word of God
C. Be Satisfied, Filled

2. A Gift of Bread. (v. 41)
A. A Gift Freely Given
B. Comes Down from Heaven
C. God is Shared with Us

3. Well Fed. (vv. 35, 51)
A. Infinite Grace Available
B. Spiritual Gifts: Variety and Richness

94

C. Abundant Life

D. Eternal Life

4. Spiritual Anorexia. (v. 43) Anorexia is a disease characteristic of persons who are obsessed with being thin. They always think they are too fat and so refuse to eat.

    A. Denial of the Spirit. Refusal to believe that anything exists apart from the natural.

    B. One-dimensional Living. Trying to live according to one's self-interest only.

    C. Absence of Belief and Trust. Lack of nourishment for the soul.

5. Drawn by God to God. (vv. 44, 45)

    A. Exposure to the Scriptures

    B. Exposure to the Life of Jesus

    C. Exposure to the Fellowship of Believers

6. Who Has Seen God. (v. 46)

    A. Jesus Makes God Visible

    B. The Vision Shared

    C. Sight Needs Insight

Contact

Points of Contact

1. Divine Wisdom. In the Old Testament understanding wisdom was a gift to be sought. Wisdom was equated with divine truth. It was more than knowledge, facts, theories or even understanding. Wisdom was to experience and know spiritual reality.

People have a longing to know the full meaning and significance of life. They have an emptiness and a void if they do not find some larger purpose than simply to exist from day to day, to live three score years and ten, or if by reason of grace, more. They want to be part of some grander scheme of things.

95

Jesus offers a vision of an existence that is not directly seen but is very real. We need not only to see that vision but also to perceive the reality that supports it. It is not sufficient to know the facts of Jesus' life: that he was born, grew, labored, was crucified, dead, buried.

People need to experience the reality of the source from which his life and teachings flow. They need to have an awareness of that presence in their life today. Jesus needs to be encountered as the embodiment of the wisdom that comes from participating in the reality itself. He claims to participate and enable those who come to him to share in it as well.

2. Eternal Life. Belief is more than giving the assent of the mind to certain facts or propositions. It means believing in Jesus Christ enough to trust that his life and teachings are based on reality, on truth.

Eternal life is the consequence of faith that real life is following Jesus. Knowing that being faithful to Jesus grants the real meaning of life results in a trust that overcomes our fears. Death is no longer something to dread. Suffering in the vale of tears can be endured for it no longer affects the destiny for which we were created.

Life is not simply a shimmering appearance that floats upon the world for a time and then disappears forever. Life is a part of the eternal being that persists beyond the brief span upon this earth. Jesus in his death and resurrection points us beyond the passing of what we know in the world of change and decay. He discloses that which is incorruptible and permanent.

3. The Bread of Hospitality. In the Middle East traditionally bread is more than mere food. It signifies the sharing of life. When a person breaks bread with another person, it signifies the sharing of life with that person. The persons who share bread together share life and have a unity that should not be broken.

Jesus understood well that meaning of life. Those who broke bread with him entered into his fellowship and could achieve a unity with him. Through him they could realize the same unity that he shared with God.

Members of the church should share that same depth of fellowship both with God in Christ and with each other. Their sharing of the symbol of bread means that they have a life in common with each other and with Christ. If they share that life together, they have a concern, a desire to sustain, protect, and nourish the lives of those who take bread with them. It gives them a sense of mutual support in which they have strength to engage in their work in the world and their continued growth into Christ-likeness.

Illustrative Materials

1. Varieties of Bread. The importance of bread as a sustainer of life can be found in the varieties of bread. It can vary by the staple from which it is made: whole grain, barley, white flour, rye, cornbread, shortbread, enriched bread, carrot bread, pumpkin bread.

It can vary by what is added to it: fruit bread, nut bread, raisin bread, sweet bread, garlic bread.

It can vary by the shape given to it: round, square, French, Italian, buns, rolls, croissants.

2. Turkey Red Wheat. The hard wheat from which a high quality flour is made has an interesting history. Mennonites lived in the Ukraine, a part of nineteenth century Russia. Because of their opposition to war arising from their Christian faith, they decided to emigrate when Russia introduced military conscription. As families packed to leave, they selected the best of their Turkey red seed grain and filled a trunk to take with them.

When the Mennonite refugees migrated to the prairie provinces of Canada and the plains states of the United States, they brought the seed with them and found the prairie land receptive. From these trunks of wheat have come the hard flour that is preferred for many purposes over the soft wheat which was the only kind available earlier. This wheat made the prairies a breadbasket that has shipped wheat and flour all over the world.

3. Sliced Bread. How often have you heard the expression that something is the greatest thing since sliced bread? Everyone knows the convenience and uniformity of having the bread already sliced. Earlier, when people sliced their own, they often had difficulty getting it right. But nothing has excelled the greatest thing since Jesus offered himself as the bread for life!

4. A Supporting Fellowship. Germaine Burton of Birmingham, Alabama, was so violent and disruptive in school that he was in danger of being expelled and never graduating. He was constantly engaged in fights with other students. In the ninth and tenth grades he was sent to the library repeatedly for "solitary confinement." There he found a librarian who took a personal interest in him. To quote him, "She knew I was a better person than that." Ada Johnson would calm him down and try to persuade him not to go around fighting all the time. Her persistence and steady interest led him to reconsider how to deal with other people. Because she believed him to be better, he became better. On May 25, 1995, he expected to graduate. Her support was better than bread for Germaine. [Lynn Menton Reports, "Fresh Reports: 'She Knew I Was a Better Person than That.'" *Parade Magazine*, May 4, 1995, p. 20.]

5. Sugar and Starch. A report from the Center for Science in the Public Interest criticizes baby food as too laden with starches and sugar. Though the foods are not dangerous in themselves, they are overloaded with water, thickeners and fillers. As a consequence, the babies do not get the proper nutrition values from the foods at the price that is charged for them. [Report in *Toledo Blade*, April 2, 1995, p. 3.]

Does our television diet for children give too much sugar and starch and not enough wholesome bread for their diet?

7. Eating Living Bread

John 6:51-58

---

[51] *"I am the living bread that came down from heaven. Whoever eats of this bread will live forever; and the bread that I will give for the life of the world is my flesh."*
[52] *The Jews then disputed among themselves, saying, "How can this man give us this flesh to eat?"* [53]*So Jesus said to them, "Very truly, I tell you, unless you eat the flesh of the Son of Man and drink his blood, you have no life in you.* [54]*Those who eat my flesh and drink my blood have eternal life, and I will raise them up on the last day;* [55]*for my flesh is true food and my blood is true drink.* [56]*Those who eat my flesh and drink my blood abide in me, and I in them.* [57]*Just as the living Father sent me, and I live because of the Father, so whoever eats me will live because of me.* [58]*This is the bread that came down from heaven, not like that which your ancestors ate, and they died. But the one who eats this bread will live forever."*

Most Americans eat well. Three square meals a day is not uncommon. Indeed, many eat five or six times a day if coffee breaks, evening snacks, and other times of eating are counted in addition to breakfast, lunch, and supper.

Drive through a town of any consequence and count the number of fast food places and restaurants that are found. At some corners of major roads or along a block or two of a busy thoroughfare you may find five to ten feeding establishments. It is not uncommon to find in close proximity McDonald's, Burger King, Burger Chef, Arby's, Subway, Pizza Hut, Domino's, Dairy Queen, Long John Silver's, Wendy's, and Taco Bell as well as lesser known or local look-a-like fast food establishments.

Go into a major supermarket and count the variety of products that are similar. The only discernible difference often is in the trade name. Whole aisles will be filled with a vast array of cereals. Another aisle will be filled with competing brands of soft drinks: Coca-Cola, Pepsi, Royal Crown, 7 Up, and lesser known or store brands.

Try to find in the same area a religious bookstore. Compare the size of the religious book and supply store with the supermarket. It does not appear that people are as eager to be fed spiritually as they are to be fed physically!

Or perhaps we should look at the churches. How do they compare with the feeding and drinking establishments? A person would have some variety of "brand names" to choose among.

John 6 takes the preoccupation of the crowds with food and drink as an occasion to move from physical eating and drinking to the more important needs of the spirit. Nourishment is needed for spiritual life and growth.

Context

Context of the Lectionary

Today's lesson from the Gospel continues, and even overlaps by one verse, last Sunday's reading. The general opinion is that the image of eating the bread in the previous lesson dealt more with the Old Testament imagery of bread as a symbol of divine wisdom. It suggests that Jesus is the source of divine wisdom. The reading today is more clearly using eating of the flesh and drinking of the blood as symbolic of the Eucharist.

The First Lesson. (1 Kings 2:1-12; 3:3-14) David gives his dying instructions to Solomon. He first admonishes him to walk with God and keep his instructions and commandments. Then he gives him instructions of how to deal with allies and enemies. Then the death of David is reported. The second passage tells how Solomon worships God and, when offered a blessing from God because of his faithfulness, he does not ask for riches, long life or the life of his enemies. Instead he asks for wisdom and understanding. God acknowledges the worthiness of the request and grants it.

The Second Lesson. (Ephesians 5:15-20) Paul advises the Ephesians how they should live wisely. As Solomon sought wisdom to serve God, Paul admonishes the Ephesians to show wisdom in the way they live.

Gospel. (John 6:51-58) John reports Jesus' discourse on eating his flesh as living bread and drinking his blood. He responds to a debate among the Jews about his statement and elaborates on the meaning of what he said.

Psalm. (Psalm 111) The psalmist expresses his praise to the Lord for his magnificent works. He ends with the admonition that the fear of the Lord is the beginning of wisdom. This condition is the same as the theme found in the first and second lessons.

Context of the Gospel according to John

John differs from the synoptic gospels in several respects. He does not include the baptism of Jesus by John the Baptist, though he treats the relationship of Jesus to John the Baptist. John the Baptist is presented as a forerunner of and subordinate to Jesus. At one point (John 4:1, 2) John reports that the Pharisees heard that Jesus was baptizing more disciples than John the Baptist, but that is immediately followed by the disclaimer that Jesus himself did not baptize. Only his disciples did. It is probably significant that this note is sandwiched between the account of the new birth in the conversation with Nicodemus and the conversation with the woman at the well. Jesus offers her the water that quenches all thirst.

John also has the extended account of the Last Supper as a feast of the Passover (John 13-17), but he does not have the words of institution for the Eucharist. The reading for today has echoes of the words of institution more clearly than anywhere else in John's gospel account.

For accounts of the words of institution of the Lord's Supper in the synoptic gospels, see Mark 14:22-25; Matthew 26:26-29; Luke 22:17-21. See also 1 Corinthians 11:23-26.

> Genesis 2:23-24 — The woman is flesh of the man's flesh and the two become one flesh.
>
> Joel 2:28 — The Lord will pour his spirit on all flesh.
>
> Psalm 78:25 — People ate the bread of angels and the Lord sent them food in abundance.
>
> Romans 8:9-11 — Paul speaks of being in the Spirit of Christ rather than in the flesh and through being in the Spirit having life.
>
> 1 Corinthians 3:1-3 — The Corinthians are people of the flesh as infants in Christ though fed with milk, not solid food.
>
> 2 Corinthians 2:15-17 — Paul says speaking in Christ as sent from God leads to life, not death.
>
> Ephesians 2:13-14 — Paul speaks of being in Christ Jesus by his blood and being made one in his flesh.

Content

Precis (John 6:51-58)

Jesus uses the symbol of the living bread that gives eternal life and relates it to his sacrifice of life for the world. In response to a furious debate among the Jews who are horrified at the thought of cannibalism, Jesus uses words similar to those in the institution of the Eucharist. He proceeds to assert a unity between those who eat of his flesh and drink of his blood. He makes a further connection between himself and the living God who sent him and the life he bestows on those who partake of him. He contrasts those who ate the bread in the wilderness and died with those who eat the living bread of himself and have eternal life.

Thesis: Those who partake of the living bread in Christ have eternal life.

Theme: Eating means trusting Christ; drinking means obeying Christ.

Key Words in the Parable

1. "Living Bread." (v. 51) Living bread becomes an alternative for bread of life as found in John 6:35, 48.

2. "Came Down from Heaven." (v. 51) A repetition of the theme of incarnation that is basic to John's gospel account.

3. "Give ... my Flesh." (v. 51) An allusion to the self-sacrificial death of Jesus.

4. "The Jews ... Disputed." (v. 52) The term in Greek suggests a violent dispute among the Jews. They would be scandalized by the thought of cannibalism, a charge that was sometimes made against Christians because opponents misunderstood their celebration of the Eucharist.

5. "Eat my Flesh ... Drink my Blood." (v. 54) The Aramaic had no good word for body, as opposed to the Greek which had words that distinguished between the flesh and the body. Blood frequently is identified with the life of a person or an animal since when the blood is drained life is gone. The use of flesh and blood together would indicate the full humanity of Jesus. He was no disembodied spirit that inhabited a man, as some Gnostics proposed.

6. "Because of the Father." (v. 57) Scholars disagree as to whether the term translated "because" refers to the source of Jesus' life or whether it means he lives on behalf of the Father.

7. "Your Ancestors ... Died." (v. 58) Did the Israelites only die physically in the desert, or does Jesus suggest that in their rebellion and complaining they were already spiritually dead?

Contemplation

Issues and Insights

1. The Eucharistic Implications. The emphasis seems to shift from John 6:41-51 to John 6:53-58. It is no longer believing that leads to life. It is feeding and drinking. Jesus becomes the agent of salvation by giving his life for those who came to have a unity with him. A unity of fellowship with the living Lord, indicated by eating his flesh and drinking his blood, grants true living.

The passage raises the issue of how one celebrates the Lord's Supper. Is it some kind of magical act conferred by the elements themselves? Is it a memorial to the memory of the life, death and resurrection of Jesus until he comes again? Is the breaking of the bread and the pouring of the cup a reenactment of the crucifixion of Jesus on behalf of the world? Is the act of feeding and drinking a commitment to take the substance of Jesus' life into our life so that we live the life he lived? Is it all of the above or none of the above?

2. To Whom Do We Owe Life? The concept of Jesus being sent by God and Jesus giving his life for the world raises the issue of the source and purpose of our life. Are we brought into the world for our own pleasures and purposes or are we brought into the world for a larger purpose which our lives are to serve? Jesus had a clear sense that his life was dedicated to doing the will of God. He was bound by the source of his being to show the meaning of God's character and nature. He in turn calls his followers to be bound to God through him in the same way as he was bound to God. By partaking of his nature through the action of the Holy Spirit, we are released to a larger purpose and activity.

3. Mutual Indwelling. To assimilate the Son of Man into our being means that we dwell in constant union with Christ. He becomes the motivating force that drives our life. Our entire life comes to depend on Christ. That becomes our reality of faith, worship, fellowship, obedience, and all our actions.

Our life no longer depends on our self-interest. We live on what Jesus has done for his people by his life, death and resurrection. We appropriate his virtues by absorbing his teachings, character, mind, and ways of relating to all people.

In this sense the passage is not only a reference to the celebration of the Eucharist. It is a statement of the entire life of those who are called to follow Christ. The unity with Christ is not some ethereal mystical event. It is a translation of his life into ours in a daily walk with him that becomes a life forever with him.

4. Is John Anti-Sacraments? As noted earlier, John does not have either the baptism of Jesus or the institution of the Eucharist in the Last Supper during the Passover meal. Does he deliberately omit these events? He surely must have known about them.

Perhaps John deliberately omits the record of these sacramental episodes because of abuses of them in the church of his time. In Jesus' conversation with the Samaritan woman at the well, Jesus talks about the worship of God in spirit and truth. Does John want people to get beyond the external forms of worship to the reality of relationships? He may want people to live in a real unity with Jesus as shown in their character and activities. It seems clear that the discourse found in John 6:51-58 is a discussion of the meaning of eating and drinking. The passage relates them to partaking of the flesh and blood of Jesus. Such eating and drinking becomes a sharing of the life of Jesus fully and forever.

5. To Whom Does Jesus Speak? The usual words of institution of the Eucharist at the Last Supper are found in the synoptic gospels and were addressed only to the disciples. If John 6:51-58 is John's substitute for the establishment of the Eucharist, then the words are addressed to a crowd and not just to the disciples.

Does the different setting for the discourse on eating the living bread signal that the Eucharist is not just for the disciples? It is for the entire church. Certainly John's account shows that the partaking of the life of Jesus is meant for everyone and is not restricted to a select group of disciples.

Perhaps by setting the discourse in response to a common meal rather than a more ritual Passover meal John also wants to address the issue of how often the Eucharist is to be celebrated. The early church as reported in Acts 2:46 broke bread in their homes daily. That practice moves the memory from the worship in the temple and makes it part of daily life. Christians are meant to partake of the life of Jesus as regularly as they eat food for the physical body. The manna was given daily to the Israelites in the desert. Jesus offers himself daily to his followers.

Homily Hints

1. Partaking of Christ. (v. 53)

A. Believing. The initial step one must take is to accept the life and teachings of Jesus as having authority and salvific consequences.

B. Trusting. One relies on God's help to deal with the problems of living, both internally to one's person and externally to relations with others and the larger world.

C. Obeying. Believing and trusting in the God of Jesus Christ enables a person to live faithfully in following the teachings of Jesus even when they make demands that go contrary to conventional wisdom and human prudence.

2. Flesh or Spirit. (vv. 55, 58)

A. Doing What Comes Naturally. Do we simply follow our biological impulses?

B. Doing What Comes Spiritually. Living in Christ helps us overcome natural desires and to live according to the Spirit.

C. Being Fully Human. Jesus was truly human. If we partake of his nature and character we manifest what it means to be truly human.

3. True Food. (v. 55)

A. Malnourished. Living according to false desires.

B. Undernourished. Neglecting the activities which feed the life of the spirit in Christ.

C. Fully Nourished. The life that fully understands and is committed to following Christ in all of life.

4. Where Do You Abide? (v. 56)

A. Abiding in Christ.

B. Christ Abiding in Us.

C. Abiding Forever.

5. Living Forever. (v. 58)

A. Shedding the Past. Giving up the sin and guilt that lead to death.

B. Living in the Present. Trusting God to forgive and allow us to begin anew every day in faithfulness.

C. Hope for the Future. We live without fear of all the evil forces in the world because we have a living hope for eternal life.

6. Living to Eat or Eating to Live. (v. 58)

A. Living to Eat. Pursuing the pleasures of the flesh.

B. Eating to Live. Living according to the spirit.

C. Fed to Serve. We eat to serve purposes larger than self-interest and carnal desires.

Contact

Points of Contact

1. Cookbooks are among the best-sellers of publishers. For some publishers, including church publishing houses, cookbooks are their main money-makers. Nonprofit organizations raise money by collecting local or ethnic recipes, printing them in booklet form, and selling them.

Each year magazines run feature stories in their November and December issues on menus and recipes for the holiday seasons. Then in January and February they run diet plans and articles on how to lose weight. According to a report, Americans gain an average of six pounds over Thanksgiving and Christmas. If you multiply 250 billion times six pounds, you get 1,500 trillion pounds!

If we take John 6 seriously as Christians, we should replace our preoccupation with eating and dieting with feeding on Christ. It would lead us to concern for the hungry of the world. We should follow our occupation as disciples of Christ rather than our preoccupation with eating and trying to lose excess weight.

2. Recent articles raise questions about the obsession of the medical profession with prolonging life. Doctors go to extraordinary lengths to keep a person alive even though they know that the person is dying. Too often dying is not looked upon as a natural process. Sometimes expensive processes are ordered mainly to satisfy the family that doctors are doing everything imaginable to keep the person alive when they know that the processes avail little or nothing for the patient.

Persons who have confidence in the God of Jesus Christ and know the reality of eternal life should lose their fear of death. Indeed, at the end of a long life they should welcome the relief from the pain, suffering and limitations of life in the world. To be released as part of the natural order of human existence and to experience the timelessness of life beyond the passing of the flesh is a promise filled with hope for those who trust in the God of goodness and grace.

3. The American culture has gone through a social change since World War II. Increasingly, families either have both parents employed outside the home or they have only a single parent for support. In both instances the family fills up most of its time with paid employment.

One result is that little time is left to volunteer for the tasks of the church. Women earlier provided much of the volunteer time for teaching Sunday school, quilting and sewing for missions, preparing food for fellowship meals, and other such tasks. Now they work at paying jobs and continue to do most of the household chores. They now have more money than time in many instances.

A consequence for the church is that people have little time for the life of the spirit. The church has often moved to a kind of professionalism where services are by paid employees, where earlier much was done by volunteers.

The new situation often leaves people with a hunger for time and opportunity for spiritual renewal. They need occasions for engaging in activities in which they are more consciously feeding on Christ while they are serving larger purposes.

4. The celebration of the Eucharist is a group activity. The breaking of bread together should enhance the fellowship of the church along with the fellowship with Christ. It should be an occasion for developing a sense of unity as the body of Christ.

The celebration of the Eucharist can be more than a self-indulgent ritual of seeking one's own salvation if we pay attention to those with whom we are joined in the fellowship of the Lord's meal. The unity of the body of Christ becomes real if we observe the needs of those with whom we commune and ask how we can be servants to them. If we share in the body then any part of it that is hurting becomes our hurt. Relieving the suffering of any member of the body relieves our suffering and the sufferings of Christ, as he also suffers with his body.

Illustrative Materials

1. Hunger in the World. According to statistics from Oxfam, 2,500 people will die of hunger during the typical one-hour church worship service. Two-thirds of them will be children. A third of the children in the world are very underweight for their age. About one-fifth of the people in the world are so malnourished that they cannot engage in productive activity.

The problem is not a lack of food. Enough food is produced to provide an adequate diet for everyone. A part of the problem is a matter of distribution. The food is not equally available to those who are hungry. A part of the problem also is a lack of will and a sense of priority to feed the hungry.

2. False Diets. Much of what the media in America provides is a false diet. A recent advertisement for a series of comic books for young people touts the fact that they are extremely violent. They are filled with gory details of fighting among people. Heroes are those who can wreak the most destruction and death.

A result is that though violent crime went down in 1994, crime, especially murder, has increased sharply among adolescents. Symptoms of the false diet being fed are the legislation to lower the age at which teenagers may be tried as adults and the greater punishment given where guns are used by them in committing a crime.

3. Food Pyramids. New standards for diet were proposed recently. A new food pyramid was developed as a guide for healthy eating. It includes a base of bread, cereals, rice and pasta. The next level up the pyramid is vegetables and fruit. A still smaller next level is milk, yogurt, cheese, meat, poultry, fish, eggs, and nuts. The smallest group at the top is fats, oils and sweets.

We can propose a food pyramid for those who want a healthy spiritual life. You may want to develop your own, but it might include a base of feeding on the word of God by study and meditation on the scriptures. Upon that base one is nourished by Christian fellowship. It should include servings of regular worship. To that a daily use of prayer and devotions could be added. On top of those elements should be time for Christian service to meet the needs of others.